THE WAY OF INANNA

THE WAY
OF INANNA

A Heroine's Guide
to Living Unapologetically

SEANA ZELAZO, LICSW

HANIEL PRESS

Books may be purchased through booksellers or by contacting Sacred Stories Publishing.

Cover art: *Moon Mamas*, by Madeleine Hay. All additional artwork also by Madeleine Hay.

The Way of Inanna:
A Heroine's Guide to Living Unapologetically
Seana Zelazo, LICSW

Tradepaper ISBN: 978-1-958921-07-4
Electronic Book ISBN: 978-1-958921-08-1

Library of Congress Control Number: 2022944195

Published by Haniel Press

An Imprint of Sacred Stories Publishing, Fort Lauderdale, FL

Printed in the United States of America

For my mother and sisters

Inanna placed the *shugurra*, the crown of the steppe, on her head.

She went to the sheepfold, to the shepherd.

She leaned back against the apple tree.

When she leaned back against the apple tree,

her vulva was wondrous to behold.

Rejoicing at her wondrous vulva,

the young woman Inanna applauded herself.[1]

Contents

We shall not cease from exploration
And the end of all our exploring
Will be to arrive where we started
And know the place for the first time.
Through the unknown, remembered gate
When the last of earth left to discover
Is that which was the beginning…

—T.S. Eliot, *The Four Quartets*[2]

Preface

As the first epic myth ever recorded, *The Descent of Inanna* reads like a Divinely charted map to guide us back to ourselves—to the truth of our origins. Understanding our roots can help us find our highest evolutionary expression.

The Descent of Inanna was written in cuneiform on clay tablets dating back to around 1750 BCE, although it may have existed in some form even before then. The clay tablets containing the myth were recovered in the Sumerian site Nippur, near the modern city of Baghdad. The first excavations were conducted between 1889–1900; numerous fragments were pieced together by scholars, archeologists, and Sumerologists over approximately the next 100 years. Further study and elucidation continue, but the most comprehensive and accessible version to date appears in Diane Wolkstein and Samuel Noah Kramer's 1983 collection *Inanna—Queen of Heaven and Earth: Her Stories and Hymns from Sumer,* which is based on Kramer's translation.

The heroine of the story is the Sumerian goddess Inanna, the Goddess of Love and War. In early Roman culture, Inanna was known as Venus; in Greece, she was called Aphrodite. In Mesopotamian mythology, she is Ishtar, and in Canaanite myths, Inanna is Astarte. When I first read about her, I felt bowled over by a soul-level recognition, as if Inanna were reaching out from history to get my attention. Inanna's message of heart-centered wisdom is one of unapologetic authority and urgency.

Inanna's commitment to restoring humanity no doubt began with the great flood. The Sumerian myth, *The Deluge*,[3] contains revelations about the Sumerian origin story of humanity and its cosmology, as well as a story of the flood that destroyed the land and lasted for seven days and nights. This particular myth was contained on a single cuneiform tablet that was originally published in 1914 by the German Assyriologist, Arno Poeble[4].

Although the tablet is broken, the lower third is well preserved. In his book *History Begins at Sumer: Thirty-Nine Firsts in Recorded History*, Sumerologist Samuel Noah Kramer describes *The Deluge* text, helping us make sense of the overall story even while some lines are missing. After we learn in the text of five antediluvian cities that were created, he writes, "A break of about thirty-seven lines follows next; these must have dealt largely with the decision of the gods to bring the flood to destroy mankind."[5]

In the preserved section, Inanna is clearly distraught over this decision, and she sets up a lament and begins mourning humanity. Kramer continues: "When the text becomes intelligible again, we find some of the gods dissatisfied and unhappy over the cruel decision."[6] We can imagine Inanna observing the aftermath and pledging never to let it happen again.

The power of Inanna has returned to insist that we live in unity consciousness, to restore balance to the planet and ourselves. She invites us to take responsibility and reclaim our role as masterful creators, alchemists like herself, to weave a new paradigm for living that vibrates at the frequency of love. We must act now to integrate the wisdom of the heart in order to bring about the healing, equilibrium, and restoration our world needs—and we must begin by transforming ourselves. Let us celebrate her commitment to humankind and her pledge to help us remember our own goddess nature. Inanna's myths reveal her mission to live as an expression of the Divine and demonstrate to others how to self-actualize toward this end. Central to her own path is her devotion to uplifting everyone around her.

Today, her energy returns in the spirit of restoration, urging us to dismantle oppressive master narratives, including patriarchy and all forms of exclusion based on race, gender, and disability—hate-based thinking that is destroying humanity and our precious planet. Inanna is encouraging us to start by healing ourselves and reconnecting with our Divinity. In doing so, we can counter the imbalance on Earth and avoid the near-annihilation we experienced at the time of the great flood.

As a goddess who is fully actualized and integrates her polarities, Inanna is characterized by her embodiment of all stages of the evolutionary process including birth, death, and rebirth. She personifies both chaos and order and the light and darkness of her moon lineage. Balancing paradoxes is integral to our transformation. Inanna's intention is to help us access our own sense of empowerment so that, ultimately, we can be our own guides. It is to this end that we have written this book. I say "we" because Inanna's voice imbues this manuscript. The words transcribed herein function as a portal into the energy of Inanna herself.[7]

In ancient Sumer, the temples of the patron gods and goddesses of each city were considered their actual home on the Earth plane. It was believed that these gods and goddesses would embody the statues made in their likeness, which were sacred and revered. Sumerians treated the effigies themselves as Divine, leaving offerings of appreciation. Like those carved statues in Sumer, may the art of the written word within these pages also embody Inanna, bringing her into this physical world to connect with you directly.

HOW THE BOOK WORKS

Written to reintroduce readers to the wise and unapologetic teachings of Inanna, this book is also a portal to the temple of Inanna—a sanctuary of healing. The book begins with my personal experience with Inanna, followed by a genealogical overview outlining the Sumerian creation myth and Inanna's lineage and family constellation. This background orients the reader with the groundwork for the transformative process that follows. A description of how the patriarchy attempted to eradicate the Divine Feminine and why it must be restored also helps readers understand the urgency of the message herein.

Each subsequent chapter documents one of Inanna's most impactful and life-altering stories. Unlike the teachings of the Abrahamic religions of the modern world, Inanna's stories were written directly from the hand of the poets and temple scribes of Sumer on clay tablets that have been translated directly. The words have not been altered, and they reach us as they were intended to be read. This fact is particularly significant for the healing of feminine consciousness, which has long been traumatized by and filtered through the patriarchy.

Much of our recorded history has been reframed through the agenda of patriarchal rule. The history we have been taught was written by those in power who edited it to align with their views. For example, the Old Testament was written more than 500 years after the Exodus, while the New Testament was composed by the orthodox Christian majority. As such, only what fit their patriarchal agenda was included. In *Christo Paganism: An Inclusive Path*, Joyce and River Higginbotham explain:

> Those (stories) in which women played prominent ecclesiastic roles were not included. Those that urged the

authority of personal experience over the authority of priest or bishop were left out. Essentially the books that supported orthodox view and the power of the institution were kept while those that did not were rejected.[8]

The Sumerian texts, by contrast, were not rewritten with an agenda. They were simply discovered and delivered to us directly through the care, diligence, and commitment of archeologists the world over.

This book is an extension of my private practice as a licensed psychotherapist and former hospice social worker and spiritual coach. My aim here, as it is in my practice, is to facilitate the reader's ability to adopt an empowered perspective and pure vibration of unconditional love of self, humanity, and the planet. The preliminary work of the initial section of this book enables the self-transforming protocols in the subsequent seven chapters.

Inanna's stories are examined alongside an analogous challenge from our current reality, a reality that may be blocking us from remembering our Divinity. Considered alongside Inanna's mythic trajectory, these common contemporary provocations symbolically mirror aspects of Inanna's initiatory process, thereby underscoring the interwoven nature of reality across time and space and helping us to process the here and now. The seven chapters are modeled after the seven gates that Inanna confronted on her own journey and act as seven levels of initiation. These seven gates are also linked to the seven chakras of the body.[9] Importantly, each of these spiritual centers has a corresponding psychological characteristic. Thus, the process of navigating this book is a protocol for confronting the seven gates of your own initiation, both spiritually and psychologically.

My use of myth in this book depends on and is enriched by a contemporary context, as is its relationship to the chakra system, celebrating the generative plasticity of new and alternative perspectives. Inanna is all about honoring who you are and where you are. The book does not, therefore, move linearly through the chakras, because life is not linear.

The book begins with Inanna's descent in Gate One and ends with her ascent in Gate Seven. The myths and hymns retold in between do not follow Inanna's chronological age, either. Indeed, her descent and subsequent ascent happen later in her life than in the other stories, and this anachronism is intentional. It highlights the circular nature of our path as human beings and the simultaneity of our energetic experiences.

Each gate offers a healing intervention at the end to support your movement through the respective challenges. In the vein of Inanna's alchemical lineage—including her grandfather Enki, who was the God of Wisdom and a master alchemist—the interventions are transformational and comprise a spiritual approach based on ritual, ceremony, meditation, and prayer. The process is informed by transpersonal psychology and a strengths-based focus, providing you with concrete tools to reclaim your own unapologetic, Divine nature. By combining the spiritual and psychological, we bring healing to our bodies and move into balance. As we do this individually, we alter the collective vibration and bring healing to the body of Mother Earth herself.

The exercises listed throughout are intended to align with the pacing set by your higher self. Trust the process. Having a sacred journal to accompany you on this journey is useful. Think of the journal as a talisman that will allow you to integrate this undertaking. I encourage you to treat the selection of your journal as a ritual. Ask Inanna to help you align with the ideal energetic match and to choose a journal that aligns with your needs and goals. Make it your own. Get creative. You might want to decorate it to look and feel like the holy instrument it will become for you—an instrument to document your journey with Inanna and the extraordinary transformation that will ensue. When you revisit your entries upon completion, you will surely be inspired!

It is my hope that you fall in love with this Goddess of Love and that she helps you open your heart unconditionally so that you may learn to live as one. When you reclaim oneness, you assist in restoring balance within and without, thereby helping the collective to heal and allowing us all greater access to experience Heaven on Earth.

May Inanna help you own your power. May she lead you to fall madly in love with yourself. May she remind you to live unapologetically as the radiant being that you are. May it be so.

How Working with Inanna Transformed Me

As you will soon see, the process of working with Inanna is very individual. However, by offering my own process, I hope to contextualize what is possible and how it might look in the everyday.

I *fell* into Inanna. During my research into the Divine Feminine, I was catapulted into my own descent through the Great Below, where I came crashing into Inanna. Immediately, I felt her power.

When I told one of my teachers that I was writing this book, she asked in jest, "Are you going to put a warning label on it?" My journey with Inanna began several years ago when she helped me remember the truth of who I am. She electrified parts of me I've long been waiting to activate.

Her timing, of course, was Divine. As a younger woman, I'm not sure I would have been able to manage the directness of her force. I would likely have resisted her. Now I know we found each other at exactly the right time.

HEALING THE LINEAGE

Inanna taught me what self-love looks like. It had been an intellectual concept that I had been successfully helping people to access in my private psychotherapy practice for years—as well as later in my work as an intuitive channel—but I had yet to embody it as a lived experience. Until I made my reconnection with Inanna, I understood self-love as something I could help others achieve.

Like many of us, I was challenged throughout my life with an inability to love myself unconditionally. In part, this was due to how prominent self-abuse was in my family. It was passed down to me directly from my own mother's struggle and her mother's struggle before that. My mother was my guide for womanhood. And yet she struggled with having faith in herself.

THE WOUNDING THAT LED TO MY CONNECTION TO INANNA

My own initiation began when I was nineteen. It started in the middle of the night as I was working on my final paper for an American Literature class at McGill University. I was writing an essay on Kate Chopin's novella *The Awakening*. The heroine in the story takes her own life by drowning, after having spent the summer falling in love and learning to swim.

My paper explored how the protagonist literally and figuratively took her life back into her own hands through the act of suicide. At the time, I did not understand that the ocean was symbolic of the womb in which the heroine birthed herself anew in learning to swim. Significantly, in the goddess tradition, this womb became her tomb through suicide.

I pulled an all-nighter to finish the essay and walked, bleary-eyed, to the English department just in time to hand it in. When I got back to my apartment, because my blinds were still drawn, the darkness was lit up by the blinking red light on my phone. This was back when we only had land lines. It seemed too early to have a message—immediately, the red light felt like an alarm to me.

I must have played back that message ten times before I grasped what was being said. My father's voice, distressed and drained, conveying the impossible reality that my mother was in the hospital in a coma, having attempted suicide. The essay I had just written mingled with his words across time and space and contexts.

For nine weeks she was in a coma. During that time, she was moved to the Royal Victoria Hospital and into a room that overlooked the track where I practiced with the McGill team. Somehow, I walked forward during those days, one foot in front of the other, as family members and friends came into see her.

Even today I can vividly recall images of my mother from her hospital bed and how strikingly her body transformed. Spasticity had set in and her hands began to curl; we had to put rolled face cloths in her palms to try to offset this. As a nurse herself, she had told me many times that she believed that comatose patients can still hear, so I spoke to her aloud and also psychically—because ours had always been a strongly telepathic connection.

From the first day I sat at her bedside, I knew she wasn't going to wake from her coma. Given that my brother and twin sister lived in Toronto, there was just my father and my older sister Kirsten nearby to hold vigil regularly. Kirsten had a traumatic relationship with hospitals, which made it extremely uncomfortable for her to visit. Most of the time it was me and my father there.

It was my nineteen-year-old self and my father who had to decide about keeping her on life support or "pulling the plug" when the doctors told us we needed to choose. All my life, my mother had told me she never wanted to be on life support. She'd witnessed the process many times, working as a nurse. I knew this to be a truth of hers, but I had to help my father understand that.

Several days passed. Then, exactly nine weeks from her admission, with my father and me on either side of her, each holding one of her hands, my mother took her last breath. I watched as a silver energy moved from her solar plexus up across her face and out through her crown chakra. I had an intuitive sense of how to guide her soul into the Light, which I did while I continued to hold her hand. I whispered directions to her departing soul as she transitioned. I slipped a silver ring from her finger onto my own, and I have held it dear for its energetic connection to my mother ever since.

My first gate was all about the fourth chakra, the heart chakra, because of my mother's suicide. At this gate, I had to resolve profound grief. I had to work through the reductive and problematic messaging of the experience, which deconsecrated the role of mother as one in which you might lose yourself in prioritizing the needs of others ahead of your own. I had to upgrade the erroneous beliefs that were established as a result of this experience, including the belief that being a woman in this world is unbearably hard, especially for those who are sensitive.

I also had to gain the tools to neutralize internalized oppression so that rather, than leading to an annihilation of self, oppression might prompt a discovery of potent inner resources. The process led to a shattering of my heart and supreme grief, but it was also a catalyst to study and understand death and dying. Going forward, I would see that while death is a physical transition, my life's work really is about helping people negotiate transition in all ways. Being well-versed in the mystery of death prepared me for this work.

In addition, my experience deepened my access to what resides beyond the physical, into the dimension of Spirit. While still in a coma, my mother showed me psychically the emotional pain that had led to her decision, the felt sense of hopelessness she experienced. I saw the way substance, in particular alcohol, had intensified this pain for her. She also shared with me, psychically, what she had experienced before slipping into a coma. She showed me the whole horrifying process, but it was this revelation that led to profound understanding for me.

The drug she had injected into her leg finally began to take effect while she was in the kitchen of the house I grew up in, on Montreal's West Island. She had prepared her last supper, which she was about to consume when the drug started to wind up her spine, causing her to collapse on the kitchen floor. She managed to get upstairs to my twin sister's childhood bedroom. And there she closed her eyes to drift off to what she hoped would be an escape.

But that is not what happened. Instead, she slipped into a coma, and her spirit escaped from her physical body. She showed me herself in astral form, standing next to the bed, looking down at her physical body under the maroon-colored comforter. Her eyes were closed, her heart rate plummeting. To her great shock, the poignant experience of anxiety, inner judgment, depression, desperation, and hopelessness was still present— even though she was now outside and separated from her body.

What she was conveying to me was that she did not achieve the escape she was looking for. Instead, she also felt the grief of her loved ones and the karmic implications therein. Because of all of this, her pain was intensified. And that caused my nineteen-year-old self even more heartbreak.

She showed me that she was instantly met by her own guide, which I saw as a bright blue, androgynous being. This guide told her it was not yet time to leave her body fully. Then she was taken through a process with her guide, which was not revealed to me. The image I was given clairvoyantly was that she was *embraced* by her own guide. It literally appeared to me as if she was enveloped in blue light. She was able to show me this even while lying in a coma in her hospital bed.

She was assisted by her spiritual guide in a powerful process of healing. This process was clearly a rebirth; it was literally nine gestational weeks from the day of her initial hospitalization to her last breath.

As my mother went through her rebirth into a new dimensional reality, I found myself in a process of my own symbolic death. There was an energy at play that was akin to the one seen in *The Descent of Inanna*, where Inanna's corpse hanging on a nail is juxtaposed against the moaning of labor pains by her sister Ereshkigal laying on the floor. I was suddenly without ground to stand on, falling fast.

DOWNWARD SPIRAL

The next gate I confronted was the gate of the second chakra. Deep wounds that need healing often present in this sacral area. These were wounds long stored within my cellular memory of sexual violation in many past lifetimes. Those experiences needed to be transmuted energetically. This is my intuitive understanding of why I had to go through what I did next. As I entered this gate, up came fear, shame, insecurity, and deep feelings of being tainted.

I had just finished a day shift at the restaurant in downtown Montreal where I was bartending. It was six p.m. in mid-June and my purse was full of cash from happy hour. My job was situated neatly between corporate offices filled with folks ready to spend money on cheap beer and shots as soon as they were off the clock.

As I walked home to my apartment, my head was spinning from the smoke in the bar and the shock of my mother's recent death. I was shattered, a vacant hole of my former self, but I remember the bright yellow, floral sundress I had put on in an attempt to offset my inner landscape.

Several blocks from my apartment, a man approached me, speaking French. He explained that he could see I had a darkness around me. I felt it, of course. I knew it was there—but how could he see it? I thought I was a master of smiling through pain. Immediately and instinctively, I rubbed my thumb against the ring I had taken from my mother's hand only a week before. He told me that in his culture, they had a tradition of hanging masks in the home to ward off evil and darkness. He said he could sell me one.

I wanted protection. I felt so vulnerable. So, in a haze, I responded that yes, I would follow him to his place to purchase a mask. The summer sun was still in the sky and the streets were filled with crowds walking from campus into town. Yet I fell under a sort of spell as he guided me to the threshold of his apartment. As the door closed loudly behind me, I felt a sudden surge of panic. As he reached for a black, wooden mask hanging on his wall, I told him I had changed my mind and that I wanted to leave.

But this was not what happened; I had walked right into a dark abyss, and it engulfed me.

I remember telling my therapist, several years later, that I had been forcibly sexually assaulted at age nineteen. I said, "Yeah, so this happened, but I can't talk about it. I just want you to know it happened." I was not ready to share, to divulge the horror that filled my veins. I just wanted it to be over it, to be done. I wanted to be beyond it. I wanted to imagine it had never happened. I was afraid that if I talked about it, it would become more terrifying. I just wanted to forget it.

In hindsight, I realize that I had worn my darkness, grief, and vulnerability like a sign, and someone who had an orientation to have power over another saw that, and pounced. For me, it was a double rape. My own body was violated, but my faith in Spirit was violated, too. I was lured into this terrible situation because I believed that he could help me, since he could see my pain. This was my first experience—in this lifetime—of someone using intuitive gifts to manipulate, wield power over, and violate another.

In many ways, the experience led me to solidify my boundaries and focus on grounding and protection. Once safely home, I threw away the dress, even though it had been one of my favorites. I never wanted to see it again. A few weeks after the rape, I saw my perpetrator through the window of the bar where I was working. I wanted to throw up. I ran into the kitchen to hide, hoping he didn't see me.

I wasn't able to discuss the attack with anyone and I never reported it to the police, because I was in so much pain at that time that I didn't want it to be real. I wanted to leave it as part of the bad dream that summer had become. I wanted to wake up and feel clean. I wanted to erase the part of me I believed had become tainted.

I was also deeply ashamed. I was terrified to tell anyone because, after all, I had willingly walked right into it. I was afraid that this would make it seem consensual and that I would therefore feel worse after sharing my story. I was afraid that folks would call me gullible, unwise, an idiot. That they would say that my belief in the goodness of humanity was somehow wrong.

Just when I needed faith, the assault tore my faith to pieces. I had prayed so deeply for relief from grief; it was impossible to comprehend that the protection I sought, through my post-traumatic haze, had actually caused this unbearable violation.

My sense of safety—and in many ways, my world view—were destroyed. I locked this feeling away through repression as best I could for several years. But once safely in a relationship with my then-husband, I started to feel ready to begin letting it emerge—to allow it to come up from its burial ground, deep in my soul, for healing. I dealt it with it the only way I knew how to at the time. I resurrected my competitive spirit and took to the pavement. I hired a coach and set my goals on a marathon.

As my fitness returned and my body became leaner, I found myself working through this particular gate with some ambivalence. Races were won and records were broken, and my sights were set on an elite level. I crossed the tenuous line of committed athletic discipline into extreme rigidity. This attitude served me well in my pursuit of athletic excellence, but it came at a tremendous cost.

I was no longer running toward myself but away from myself. I set a goal to qualify for two Olympic trials. I trained long and hard. My coach was known in the sport as a "high-mileage coach." This suited me well. One hundred-mile weeks were the perfect medium in which to escape and run fast, really fast, away from myself and my womanhood.

Ultimately, I accomplished my athletic goals, but I had lost my connection to the Divine Feminine within and was completely out of balance.

MY INITIATION WITH INANNA

My grieving process led me to reframe my mother's suicide as an activation of the healer archetype in me and to remember my calling. It reinforced my connection to working in and through the in-between, the liminal, and to help others move through transition with grace.

I would switch universities and go on to major in Thanatology, which is the study of death and dying. I would train in many healing modalities, including bodywork, energy work, shamanic healing, and psychosynthesis. I'd get an MSW to work as a hospice social worker, dedicating years to helping others move through death with greater ease.

Everything about my first initiation connected me to Inanna even before I remembered her. Inanna began her initiation with the Death Mysteries, just as I had. My first gate was an opportunity to fortify my heart for the work I was called to do. Silently, and in the shadows, Inanna walked by my side. My heart had been shattered in order to be rebuilt with the strongest integrity. Going forward in the world, I would use my heart in the way Inanna does, as the instrument through which I could endeavor to offer compassionate service and be tuned to the highest vibration.

My second gate was all about the second chakra, the sacral chakra, and the way that both past-life and current-life violations of this creative center led to a sense of feeling tainted. This feeling was so powerful that I had deep, unresolved guilt around nourishing the body that had been "defiled." I also had ambivalence about my sexuality and my womanhood as a result, which led to a coping mechanism of running, both literally and figuratively, to avoid my emotions.

Sadly, I was really good at this. I stopped menstruating. It took receiving a diagnosis of osteopenia due to years of amenorrhea to call my attention to address and heal this internalized guilt about nourishing myself. So much of me felt undeserving of sustenance and love, as if I were walking around with a scarlet letter that highlighted my perceived impurity at the hands of unholy violation.

I had internalized the cultural oppression of women's physicality and the implication of its dangerous worthlessness. I heard that message and decided my own body was not even worth nourishing. I also needed to punish myself; I became my own internalized task master for my physical pursuits.

Doing anything gentle for myself, anything nurturing, anything life-giving, brought up feelings of guilt. I felt bad for taking up space and had successfully whittled down the space my body required in the world. By becoming amenorrhoeic, I had depleted my life-force blood, believing on some level that the power of the feminine consciousness was too dangerous.

In my erroneous belief system, I thought it was the presence of the regenerative feminine energy within me which led to me being defiled. This was what the patriarchy wanted to control and violate. I harbored the ancestral beliefs and pains of the women in my maternal line; I felt them all, and so I turned that feeling off as best I could through starving myself, running from myself, and not feeling anything at all.

My coping mechanism was that I was the hardest on myself, so anything that came at me from outside couldn't possibly hurt as much. Even while I was able to accomplish certain goals and dreams I had in sports, my foundation was symbolically eroded. My womanhood dried up through an unconscious belief that, without it, I would not feel my wounding.

After countless years of dedication to various therapeutic modalities in pursuit of balance and healing, it was the force, power, and wisdom of Inanna that helped me heal fully and step into unconditional love of self. She alone brought me back into myself. In remembering her, studying her, working with her, and allowing her energy to support, initiate, and guide me, I have arrived at my most balanced version of myself.

Inanna led me to fall in love with myself as I fell in love with her. She has brought me fully into congruence—the congruence she encourages, as only the Goddess of Love can.

EROTIC HEART

I see Inanna more like a partner than as a goddess I revere from afar. My devotion to her feels like that of a lover. It is an erotic connection that is about having a passion for living and loving everything and all. This is undoubtedly her way to lead me to loving myself fully from a place of devotion. I come alive when I drop into the energy of Inanna. I feel more electric; I feel the pulsing energy of intense attraction to another. And this energy then gets turned inward to self. This is a unique power I have not yet found in other goddesses with whose energies I work.

Through Inanna, I remembered myself upon the ritual altar as a high priestess in sacred union, anointing my beloved. I have *felt* my power, my mastery, my skill. I know this is true because she is the Goddess of Love. This activation and healing of my second chakra is understandable.

She burst my second chakra wide open and helped me let go of whatever restrictions were present therein. In so doing, she has helped me to figure out what I really want. She has helped me understand the desires and appetites that I have spent decades trying to figure out on my own and have explored through countless therapeutic interventions. It is as though she single-handedly resuscitated my second chakra, and that led not just to an enhanced sensuality in me, but also a deeper understanding of how to let myself play, access joy, and experience pure fun—and to do it unapologetically.

NO LONGER SORRY

I used to apologize for everything. I never wanted to be an imposition. I have even felt sorry simply placing an order at a restaurant because, having worked in the industry, I know how hard customers can be on the staff. I have said "sorry" for things that had nothing to do with me. Once a man rode his surfboard right into me while I was paddling out into the lineup, and I was the one who said I was sorry. I actually felt badly for being in the way!

Inanna has shifted this tendency in me entirely. I do not feel the need to apologize for taking up space in the world, for being smart, or athletic, or strong, or successful. I had worked on this issue for decades in therapy, with little progress. It took only a matter of months for that to shift with the power of Inanna. Her power and capacity are exceptional. I hope that connecting with her may have a similar effect on you.

THE GODDESS'S PERSPECTIVE

Inanna shifted my perspective of myself. She inspired and helped me to step outside of myself, pushing me toward joyful, sensual fulfillment, encouraging me to prioritize my own pleasure and supporting my process of learning what that means for me. She has led me to accept my body in all the ways it is today, so I *feel* beautiful. I am not as lean or defined as I was when I was competing in athletics. My stomach shares the story of motherhood. I have to wear my glasses more often than I don't, and the lines around my eyes reveal the life I have seen.

Yet I am not only okay with it all, but I feel more comfortable in this human form than ever before! Inanna has helped me to be unapologetically accepting of my body. She granted me the freedom I was longing for and didn't know how to access.

As a mother, she allowed me to let go of perfection. Sometimes I am the mother I want to be, and sometimes I'm not. With her help, though, I have been able to let go of judgment around this and accept my limitations, to find a way to use them to become strengths. She has helped me to welcome my paradoxes as part of my truth instead of things that made me feel incongruent in the past.

RECLAIMING MY VOICE

My journey with Inanna continues to deepen daily. One of the most significant ways my connection to this goddess has helped me is the healing of my throat chakra, allowing me to speak my truth with ease. She has encouraged me to own my self-expression with authority.

Through her, I found the inspiration and courage to finally step into my role as a writer. By stimulating and healing my second chakra, my creative center, Inanna helped unearth the artist in me that has been trying to emerge my whole life, but that I was too afraid to express. She folded her hands in prayer above my throat and, with a command, alchemically transformed the scars of thousands of years of suppression that I wore like a chain around my neck.

This book is my artistic collaboration with Inanna. She has helped me feel confident and safe enough to express myself unapologetically to the world.

How could I not fall in love with her?

Freefall: Finding Your Bearings

Gaining an understanding of the Sumerian creation myth helps put the power of Inanna in context. Although the following is a brief summary, it nonetheless outlines a history that requires some patience. See Inanna's ancestral lineage rendered visually below.[10]

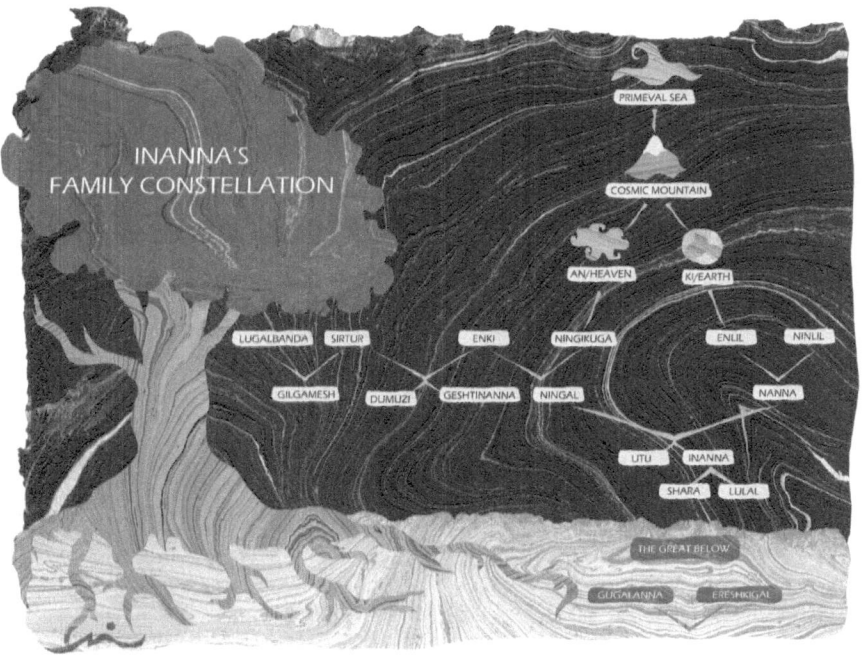

The story begins with the primeval sea, personified as the goddess Nammu—the amniotic fluid that conceived Heaven and Earth, initially united as one in its inception. Heaven was personified as the male god An; Earth, the female aspect, was the goddess Ki. The union of these two birthed the Divine child, Enlil.

For the Sumerians, Heaven was a vault which included the sky and space above the sky where the gods resided. It had a closed top and bottom. They believed the Earth was the shape of a flat disk that included the surface of Earth but also the underworld, where deities resided along with the dead. This was called the Great Below. Once Enlil separated Heaven and Earth, he and the Air Goddess Ninlil birthed the moon—the God Nanna, who also goes by Sin.[11] Nanna became one of the most significant astral gods.[12]

The additional luminous bodies in the sky came into being when Nanna, the moon god, fell in love with Ningal, a moon goddess, and they gave birth to the Sun God Utu, and to Venus—the Morning and Evening Star who was the Goddess Inanna. An and Nammu gave birth to Enlil's younger brother, Enki, the God of Wisdom and the watery deep. Enki is Inanna's grandfather; he and Ningikuga were the parents of Ningal, who was Inanna's mother. Monogamy was not a common practice among the gods and goddesses, so things can get confusing. Enki also fathered Inanna's husband, the Shepard-King Dumuzi[13] and his sister Geshtinanna, with Sirtur, a sheep goddess. Both Dumuzi and Geshtinanna figure prominently in Inanna's mythology.

In the pantheon of gods, seven gods stand above the rest in being blessed with the capacity to decree fate. These are An, Enlil, Enki, Ninhursag, Nanna, Inanna, and Utu. Each of these significant deities reigned over a specific city in Sumer where their main temple was found. Both An and Inanna were connected to the city Uruk, where Inanna's temple was located. Enlil's main temple was in the city Nippur, which was also connected to Ninlil. Enki's temple was in the city Eridu. Nanna and Ningal were the tutelary god and goddess of the city Ur.

GETTING TO KNOW INANNA

Refusing to be bound or limited in any way, Inanna is distinct from other goddesses in representing all aspects of the Divine Feminine trinity, referred to as Maiden, Mother, and Crone. Inanna represents an alternative to the binary. In fact, her tendency toward inclusion defies the limitation of either/or thinking. Instead, Inanna offers an alternative approach, characterized as she is by the tripartite attributes we will explore further throughout the book.

For example, although she is already Queen of Heaven and Earth, Inanna's journey to the Great Below grants her mastery over the Death Mysteries and she comes symbolically to reign supreme over the underworld, gaining access to the wisdom of totality. This represents the energy of the Crone.

We see her as Maiden in the myth *The Courtship of Inanna and Dumuzi*, a story of her blossoming connection with her beloved, and as Mother in *Inanna and the God of Wisdom*, wherein she acts as the guiding mother to her people by sharing with them the gifts and power she has acquired from Enki. Inanna is capable of moving between these three aspects of feminine wisdom with ease, acting as a gateway between them.

One of Inanna's most recognized emblems is the reed post, a tall pole with a loop at the top. This may be a reference to her maternal lineage, as her maternal grandmother Ningikuga's epitaph was "reed lady." Usually depicted as a pair, these reed posts could hold a rolled-up mat between the loops which could be lowered or raised as a doorway, capturing the liminality that Inanna represents.

The myths depict Inanna as a goddess who bears no shame in sharing all parts of herself. She does not hide her emotions and is consistently courageous and willing to pursue whatever compels her. She does so with urgency. Indeed, patience is not her strongest suit. Inanna seeks her full actualization and is committed to this process, regardless of what is required. She is a personification of the Divine in the material world of form and electrifies matter with the spark of both chaos and order in every moment. She is the paradox that mirrors nature and the energy of the Cosmos.

Inanna is also known as a goddess of both rain and thunderstorms. The force and potential destruction of thunderstorms is in stark contrast to the gentle replenishing nature of rain. This contrast characterizes Inanna perfectly.

LEADING HER LION

The animal associated with Inanna is the lion, and we might imagine it to be her totem. She is often depicted in artwork, poetry, or in myths with her foot resting upon a lion's back, or riding a lion, or driving a chariot pulled by seven lions.[14] As we explore her stories, we will see the number seven frequently and unpack its significance. As for the image of the lion, I see its symbolism in several ways. Inanna's multidimensionality behooves multiple interpretations. The lion might represent the untamed sexual energy that Inanna chooses to ride—an emphatic statement of the ways she prioritizes her own pleasure. Sacred sexuality is, after all, one of her superpowers. Additionally, the lion might have been a symbol that the ancient thinkers believed captured the energy of power and wisdom capable of protecting the Earth, representing courage, leadership, and bravery. In this way, Inanna is a defender, guide, and protector of humanity.

Freefall: Finding Your Bearings

The images of Inanna riding through the heavens on a lion depict her in control of her destiny, and she is indeed known as a goddess who can decree the fate of her people. However, given that she is also the Goddess of Love, this positionality highlights her unrepentant prioritization of her sexual pleasure, allowing her "holy" vulva to steer the lion to great heights. She is on top, ensuring she has control over her own fulfillment.

Inanna honors her sacred vulva, which is capable of anointing her beloved just as Mary Magdalene anointed Jesus. Significantly, in communion with her beloved Dumuzi, Inanna evolves into an even more powerful expression of herself. With him, Inanna discovers how to balance the Divine Feminine and the Divine Masculine. In this, Inanna illustrates the holy alchemy of relationships. She teaches us that a sacred relationship with self is essential to mastery, and through this love of self, one gains access to a deep connection with the other, including with the beloved. Many of us need to heed this wisdom right now.

Inanna is also the Goddess of War; her lesson is that in order to have unconditional acceptance of ourselves, we must integrate and bring healing to all parts of us, including the "warring" aspects—the aggressive, angry, dominating, and often wounded aspects of the self. Embodying these aspects, Inanna is truly a Goddess of Love—one who knows that real love is about acceptance, lack of judgment, and the courage to heal.

Historically, when worshippers of Inanna engaged in rites of sacred marriage, they channeled Inanna's intoxicating prowess, allowing their bodies to become instruments of renewal for the entire community. The sacred union in these rites allowed Inanna's worshippers to actually impact, through their generative act of love, their own understanding of being one with the *creatrix* herself. This is a teaching, therefore, about our own creative involvement as collaborators in the artistic collage of reality. That union is a doorway to our Divinity.

Seeing our shadow aspects alongside the aspects we value is an important exercise. Considering visual and literary representations of Inanna in her multidimensionality can give us perspective. Inanna is often depicted with weapons on her back, symbolic of her role as a Goddess of War. This ammunition, however, can also be seen as the tools needed to pierce through illusion with discernment, helping us slay inner aggression so it may be transmuted into love. In this light, Inanna is a warrior for unity, a destroyer of separation. This highlights the fact that she is equipped with the skills of a high priestess; like a witch or a wizard, Inanna exemplifies the teachings of consciousness and fights to defend truth.

This capacity marks Inanna as a teacher of ascension, a guide for what is unfolding here and now on the planet. Ascension is the experience of raising our level of consciousness. It is the process of expanding our human experience into our most evolved, Divine expression. Ascension is often connected to the process of spiritual awakening, which is indeed a multilayered concept.

For the purpose of this book, *ascension* should be understood as the shift in consciousness unfolding now globally within humanity, moving from separation into oneness. It is a reconnection with Source energy in a movement beyond our current and denser paradigm of the third dimension, to the higher frequency of love characterizing the fifth dimension and beyond.

This is different from the use of the term in reference to Christ's ascension, wherein he took his light body with him as he left the Earth plane. In contrast, the ascension process unfolding now is, at its core, about returning to the purity of love as we transition from the lower vibration of a fear-dominant perspective into an entirely heart-centered view, to ready ourselves for mastery. Ascension is accessible by free will; we must choose it and commit to it, which requires intense dedication and training.

While on this path, you might find yourself guided from within to engage in compassionate service to spread kindness and inspire others as we rise through our unique process of purification.

As you will see, Inanna's journey reveals her personal ascension, and her process is one that we might emulate. This is the central reason that Inanna has returned at this time. A shift occurred on the Earth plane when the Mayan calendar ended on December 21, 2012. This shift marked the end of one cycle and the beginning of a new one. The process of evolution for humanity accelerated at that time, and great cosmic assistance from the higher realms began to pour forth.

Inanna is a goddess who leads the charge through her own personal example of what is possible. Let Inanna inspire you as the teacher of ascension she is.

REPETITION AS INVOCATION

Imbued with high priestess energy, the poems and myths of Inanna read like incantations—spells cast to guide the evolution of the reader. The use of repetition in her myths has this effect and is a tool to help the reader expand. If read aloud, the repetition in the myths can elicit a trance-like state which brings Inanna to life on the page and guides us into the transformation that she experiences. She *invites* us into the experience, and through the poem, engages us in the incantatory experience.

The sacred connection to our own bodies is one of Inanna's central teachings. Much like a tuning fork, Inanna's use of repetition aligns us to our own bodies. This effect resonates with the reader deeply and enhances our connection to her. Her message reminds us that the body is the vehicle that we chose in this life to experience the teachings of the physical world.

Bringing our consciousness fully into this body allows us to tune into our souls.

Our bodies deliver critical sensory messages to us all the time, but many of us are disconnected from them and fail to hear these messages until the volume gets very loud, sometimes even creating an injury or illness. Inanna reminds us to connect with our bodies so we may receive the benefits they contribute to our spiritual evolution. In order to come into balance as a collective—so that both we and Mother Earth can heal—we must connect with our bodies and reconcile what has led to the separation.

PRESERVING THE FUTURE THROUGH POETRY

Some of the clearest and most thorough depictions of Inanna come from the poet Enheduanna, who was also a high priestess of Ur, the Sumerian center of civilization. Enheduanna lived and wrote between 2285 and 2250 BCE and was the first known writer to have signed her name to her own work. She was also personally devoted to the goddess Inanna, with whom she felt a direct relation—seeing herself as an expression of the goddess on Earth while Inanna reigned from above, below, and within all.

Enheduanna was a social activist, spiritual warrior, and transformational artist. Like Inanna, she was a powerful wisdom keeper and agent of change. Through her platform as high priestess and poet, Enheduanna propelled the cultural recognition and valorization of Inanna above all the other gods and goddesses during her time. We know of Enheduanna's great popularity given the number of copies of her work unearthed in various locations. Additionally, she was a princess. Her father was King Sargon of Akkad, who appointed her high priestess of the moon god Nanna. Her work was influential in scribal schools in Sumer.

Nevertheless, Enheduanna was from a family of males insistent on domination. In contrast to peaceful co-existence, domination was associated with the patriarchal warrior cultures that eventually overtook the Goddess in all her forms. This was the type of culture that Enheduanna was part of, even while her father felt indebted to Inanna, in her Akkadian iteration as Ishtar, for his military success.

King Sargon conquered and controlled all of southern Mesopotamia, reaching into Syria, Anatolia, which is the modern-day Turkey and western Iran. He is recognized as the founding father of the Mesopotamian military and as the first builder of an empire. Enheduanna's cousins and uncles were instated to govern the areas that King Sargon took over.[15] Their reign contributed to the demise of the goddess culture as Sargon's military domination overtook the traditional Sumerian culture that had previously reigned.

Enheduanna's creative work and her position of power became the foothold for her own valiant attempt to stave off the patriarchy and keep the Goddess alive. A prolific writer, her body of work unearthed thus far includes three long poems written to Inanna, three poems to Nanna, and forty-two temple hymns. Undoubtedly, other texts were destroyed at the hand of the patriarchy. However, in these works, we see an expression of Inanna fleshed out completely. She is raw and realistic. She will not be confined and defies strict categorization, including the binaries of gender and sexuality, of matter and spirit.

Inanna is one of the first deities recorded to have given gender fluidity a sacred place in her temple, celebrating the non-binary as regal and holy, using her platform as Queen of Heaven to teach inclusivity, unity, acceptance, and freedom. She is all that is. The range of her epitaphs— as Goddess of Love and War, of Heaven and Earth, of the Morning and

Evening Star—capture her multiplicity and multidimensionality and provide inspiration for us to explore our own plurality.

Sumerians held monthly celebrations to honor the multidimensionality of Inanna. In addition to the New Moon Feast highlighting her connection to the lunar cycles, the most prominent celebration of Inanna was the lengthy New Year celebration related to fertility rites, and the annual ritual of *hieros gamos* or "sacred marriage." *Hieros gamos* was a ritual enacted by the high priestess of Inanna, who was a symbol of Inanna herself. She had sexual intercourse with the high priest or king, who represented Inanna's husband, the shepherd king Dumuzi. Their union welcomed fertility of the land and of humanity.

In the mythology, every six months Dumuzi is released from the underworld, and his sister Geshtinanna is allowed to take his place for half of the year. The sacred sexual union between Inanna and Dumuzi was symbolically reenacted to mark the seasons of crop growth. His time in and out of the underworld corresponded with the seasons during which the land was abundant and when it was sun-scorched and devoid of growth. It is important to emphasize that Inanna acts as a catalyst, returning Dumuzi to life through her own power, vitality, and womb energy. In other words, she has a direct hand in his resurrection; as we explore in Gate Seven, we will see her role in his death as well.

Indeed, in the myths and hymns about Inanna, it is clear that her word took precedence over others and with it she was able to *command*. She reigned as queen, but like many other goddesses who came later, she was also as an oracular deity and an interpreter of dreams, especially in her earliest historical representations.

Inanna's oracular ability is perhaps most clear in her connection to the planet Venus. Among her many epitaphs, Inanna as Venus is referred to as the Morning and Evening Star. Goddess scholar Merlin Stone points out that, in some ancient Babylonian myths, Venus is referred to as Masat, which is defined as "prophetess."[16] Inanna's word was, therefore, the word of a prophetess who had direct access to and spoke the truth. This skill was attributed to many goddesses and may have been one of the reasons the Divine Feminine was vilified and decimated. Intuition, it seems, was threatening to the patriarchy. Above all, Inanna possesses the very wisdom that we, as a collective, need to restore balance, to heal, and to come to know our Divine truth.

A DEEP DIVE INTO THE DIVINE FEMININE

Before we immerse ourselves in Inanna's mythology, we must understand why her wisdom is needed so urgently and what has led to our collective imbalance. Long ago, it was believed that the origin of all humanity was female—the *Creatrix*, who gives birth to all. Goddess worship existed for more than 300,000 years. The generative, creative center of the goddess, her womb, is prominent throughout her various incarnations.

Statues of the Goddess with ample breasts, hips, and pregnant bellies were prevalent in both the Paleolithic and Neolithic cultures, highlighting the reverence held for the Divine mother of creation. There was no paternal role in governance in the clan-based systems that existed in the earliest societies. The significant male in the family system was on the maternal side, including the uncle or brother of the mother. Women were considered sacred for the womb knowledge they embodied. Throughout the natural world, it was clear that everything emerged and was born from the womb. This granted women respect, authority, and rights. Ultimately, this reverence led to the practice of matrilineal descent, wherein the lineage of kinship was through the mother line for both sexes in name, property, inheritance, and titles.

Unlike later patriarchal societies, these cultures existed without war. They were founded on the concept of balance, both men and women having specific roles within the culture but on an equal level. Sumer was a part of what is referred to as "the fertile crescent," the crescent moon-shaped area of the Middle East that was the birthplace of some of our earliest civilizations. It was the source of agriculture and irrigation as well as writing and the invention of the wheel. As such, it was also known as the cradle of civilization. The area includes ancient Mesopotamia and contains regions of present-day Egypt, Turkey, Lebanon, Palestine, Israel,

Syria, Turkey, Iran, Iraq, and Cyprus. The Nile River, the Mediterranean Sea, and the Persian Gulf surround it, and the Tigris and Euphrates Rivers run through the area.

The link between human fertility in women and the growth of crops allowed for a natural appreciation for women, inspiring them to stand fully in their power and live feeling celebrated for their gifts, including the ability to grant life. Goddess worship held strong until the Roman Christian emperors decimated the last remaining temples of goddess worship in 500 CE. But the attack on her began much earlier, as we will see below.

The Christian church not only usurped her power, but also commandeered and destroyed her temples, rebuilding their own churches over her sacred sites. The church incorporated the rites, rituals, and symbols of the Goddess, claiming them as their own and vilifying the ones that threatened them the most. For example, the snake and the forbidden fruit—both symbols of the Goddess—were recast as manipulative temptation.

Matrilineal descent involved kinship being ascribed to the mother's family line, including inheritance and titles. It allowed women to have and maintain power. As such, matrilineal descent threatened the patriarchy the most and was, therefore, a significant reason that attempts were made to obliterate the Goddess. These efforts were aimed right at the very power center of matrilineal decent, her second chakra—the life-giving womb and fulcrum of her sexuality. This was accomplished through the demonization of women's sexuality.

THE CHAKRAS AND THE DIVINE FEMININE

The chakra system is now widely known and has received much attention over the last several decades (see Figure 3: Chakra Chart, in Appendix). It refers to the seven wheels of light that move upwards through the body, beginning at the base of the spine and extending through the top of the head. The root chakra is located near the coccyx, the sacral chakra at the sexual organs, the solar plexus chakra at the stomach, followed by the heart, the throat, the third eye at the center of the forehead, and, finally, the crown chakra at the top of the head.

The sacral chakra is the center of creativity and is where we process the satiation of our appetites. It is also where we give ourselves permission to play, have fun, and experience joy. As the sexual center, the second chakra was targeted by the patriarchy who reframed the fertility practices of the Goddess as fertility cults, changing the interpretation of the holy acts therein and denigrating sacred sexual rites.

Goddess cultures differed from ours today. Sacred sexual customs were a part of life, done to support growth across the land. The priestesses who resided in the temples, for example, would engage in sexual union with those who came to worship the Goddess. Sacred sexuality was both a way to honor the Goddess and an offering the Goddess brought to humanity. These temple priestesses would choose the individual with whom they felt an attraction and engage in these rites of sacred sexuality in a deliberate ritual to ensure fertility. Adorned in their holy garments, with their chosen one at their side, they would have entered the temple. The process itself might have included using oils to anoint one another, uttering prayers or incantations to call in the Goddess, and ultimately joining in transcendent union to support the whole.

These customs were practiced and celebrated; women enjoyed a sexual freedom that it would serve us well to reintroduce. The practice of such customs was built upon religious beliefs around ensuring the perpetuation of life for all, including plants, animals, and humans. They celebrated the intuitive knowledge women had of their own bodies and how they worked. The collective feminine sacral chakra was vital and strong in goddess cultures. The sacral chakra is the center from which a woman gives birth, but it is also the center of creativity, the source through which feminine consciousness manifests in the world of form.

Feminine consciousness, or yin consciousness, is circular, receptive, unifying, unconditionally loving, non-judgmental, and compassionate. By contrast, masculine consciousness, or yang consciousness, is linear, action-oriented, driven, and willful. We need both, but we need them to be in balance, as was intended. The effects of this targeted denigration of the second charka significantly impacted us collectively.

Many of us have internalized thousands of years of oppression that has eroded our sense of confidence and self-esteem in this life and others. It has also made many women ashamed of their sexuality. Conversely, in goddess cultures where she was the patron deity of sexuality, women could connect with the Goddess through their own bodies, through their own orgasm—a devotional act that is both erotic and fulfilling. Such an intimate connection to the Goddess cultivates a holy relationship with one's own body. As a Goddess of Love, an empowering understanding of the sexual act was one of Inanna's great offerings to humanity. Inanna's return can help us to heal and restore our collective second chakra.

HOW THE PATRIARCHY ATTEMPTED TO DESTROY THE SECOND CHAKRA

The destruction happened in waves over time. In the cradle of civilization, the area known as Mesopotamia, it began with the invasion of the Indo-Europeans who came from the North and who were patriarchal and war-oriented. They were deeply threatened by the power women had in Goddess-worshipping cultures and were appalled by the sexual liberation of women. These Northern invaders began to push back against the

Goddess by maligning the women who celebrated and worshipped her, beginning around 2400 BCE. These Northern invaders maintained a view of a supreme male deity, and this influenced the mythology in the lands they overtook. Their government was structured on patriarchy instead of the matristic or matrilineal cultures of the earliest civilizations. Their introduction of male deities had a political agenda.

Later, the Hebrew and then subsequent Christian attempt to decimate the Goddess wherever she continued to reign, ultimately succeeded in subjugating her. The Hebrew and then Christian rulers changed the laws as they gained control. Adultery on the part of women was turned into a crime punishable by death. If a woman was raped, she faced death for the felony of violence against her. She was forced to be subservient to her husband, and if she wasn't a virgin or married, she was scorned.

This mentality is quite different from a culture wherein a woman could have multiple husbands and lovers. Hebrew prophets and priests began to write new doctrine declaring that all women must be officially assigned as the private property of either their father or husband. These new rules made their way into our collective unconscious and second chakra, and indeed, they profoundly impacted how women were treated and even how they felt about themselves.

When the church began to shift the balance in its hunger for power, Mother Earth and all her beings began to suffer greatly, and this continues today. St. Augustine's acceptance of original sin somewhere between the third and fourth century CE; the Burning Times in Europe from 1300 to 1800 CE; and the killing of Joan of Arc in 1431 CE all contributed to dismantling the power of the Goddess and, subsequently, the women of the world. The Bible and the Hebrew creation myth that was advanced therein had a clear patriarchal agenda. The notion that Eve caused the "fall of man" has permeated the conscious and unconscious mind of humanity, directly impacting the collective feminine for thousands of years.

It is time for us to heal. To that end, let us turn our attention directly to the Goddess of Love and War, Inanna. Her connection to humanity predates this attack on the second chakra. She is a representation of a healthy, vital, strong second chakra, capable of satiating her appetites unapologetically, and of allowing herself to have joy as well as engage her creativity. It is through her creative process that she sets up an initiation that brings her into wholeness.

To fully understand how she becomes so unapologetically herself, we must go back to the myth of Inanna's descent and explore the ways she let go of limitation to become her most empowered self.

In the following seven chapters, we observe Inanna's call to Spirit and transformation into a fully actualized being. We will begin with her most well-known myth, *The Descent of Inanna*. In the chronology of Inanna's life, her descent into the underworld comes after her myth *The Huluppa-Tree, The Courtship of Inanna and Dumuzi,* and *Inanna and the God of Wisdom*. However, because it is her call to Spirit, *The Descent of Inanna* offers a perfect organizing principle for your own process.

While it might seem counterintuitive to start with Inanna's descent into death, it is exemplary of what we will do throughout the book: come to comprehend our own significant personal experiences as initiations enabling transformation and movement to a higher level of consciousness.

Inanna's is a heroine's journey. Through reading it, you will see yourself reflected. Indeed, it is our own call to Spirit that pulls us back into remembering our truth, mission, and higher purpose. It is what lifts us out of the spiritual amnesia we experience when we come into the physical world, which causes us to forget our soul's origin. This spiritual amnesia is part of living in a third-dimensional reality. Through this call to Spirit, we awaken. We remember who we really are and can, therefore, begin our own movement toward ascension, our internal shift to embodying and living unconditional love and unity consciousness. For this reason, we begin with Inanna's descent, and through her powerful experiences, she can help equip us with the tools to rise.

Are you ready to let her guide you into the equanimity of true self-acceptance? Lay down your defenses. Inanna will accompany you the whole way. You will feel her strength beside you. Go forth with excitement into the ultimate joy that awaits you.

Gate One

THE CALL TO SPIRIT

THE MYTH

The Descent of Inanna

Inanna's ascension begins with her descent. Things to that point had been going smoothly for the Queen of Heaven and Earth. With a temple erected in her honor in seven cities, her beloved Dumuzi at her side, and devoted friends attentive to her needs and wishes, she was both powerful and comfortable.

But then she realizes that something about her situation is lacking. Compelled by an intuitive signal that comes from her soul, Inanna recognizes that she must submit to her deepest, darkest fears and descend to the underworld. An inner pressure to transform grows within her. Spirit knows Inanna is ready to understand the mysteries of the underworld, but Inanna herself is not without reservations—she cannot yet see the bigger picture. Confident in the process, however, Inanna gathers her courage and prepares to leave her holy office with its comforts and security. She gives herself over to the pull of the Great Below.

Before she goes, Inanna collects seven Divine powers: the seven *me*.[17] These are her *shugurra*, which is her crown; a single strand of lapis beads; a double strand of lapis beads; a breast plate; a gold bracelet; a lapis measuring rod and line; and her royal robe. She knows she must take these with her as the armor of a goddess. One by one, Inanna places these items on her body. Deliberately, as though engaged in a ritual, she dons her queenly apparel.

The process by which she does this is instructive. First, she places the *shugurra* on her head. She then arranges her bangs across her third eye and places her single strand lapis necklace around her throat chakra. Next, she situates her double strand of beads at her breast and dabs alchemical makeup on her eyes to enhance the allure of her gaze. Then she covers her chest with her breastplate and slips her golden bracelet over her wrist. Finally, she puts on her royal robe and picks up her measuring rod and line.

Dressed and ready, Inanna summons Ninshubur— her wise assistant, servant, and guide—to prepare a plan in case she does not come back from the underworld. Inanna knows she is venturing into a place from which no one has ever returned. Always respectful of the process of death, Inanna first instructs Ninshubur to mourn and lament her if she does not return. Following that, Ninshubur is to locate Inanna's three father figures—Enlil, Nanna, and Enki—to ask for their help in her resurrection. With this escape plan in place, she descends.

First, Inanna comes to the outer gates of the Great Below. She bangs on the door with authority, loudly declaring her presence. The gatekeeper, Neti, asks Inanna to state her reason for arrival. Still not entirely sure, she recalls the impending funeral of her sister Ereshkigal's husband, Gugalanna, deciding on the spot to state this as her official reason. Ereshkigal is the Queen of the Underworld.

Neti tells Ereshkigal about the brazen visitor, describing Inanna's powerful accoutrement in detail and depicting her breathtaking presence as larger than life. Ereshkigal cannot contain her anger, jealousy, and resentment. She is described in the myth as a petulant child who: "slapped her thigh and bit her lip" upon hearing of Inanna's arrival.[18] We assume that there must be something deeper to her response than just jealousy and, in *The Epic of Gilgamesh*,[19] we learn that Inanna had a role in the death of her husband, which we explore in detail in Gate Seven.

Ereshkigal is appalled that Inanna presumes she will be allowed to leave the underworld once she enters. As ruler of this domain, Ereshkigal pauses to consider all that Neti has told her. She listens to her intuition about what steps she must take in response. She then commands Neti to lock the seven gates to the underworld and then to prepare to unlock them one by one. She instructs Neti to force Inanna to remove one of her items at each entry point, so she ultimately arrives, "naked and bowed low"[20] without her seven powers.

Neti opens the first gate and instructs Inanna to remove her crown. He does this at each gate for each of her seven royal attributes. Once Inanna has finally gained entry, the judges of the underworld encircle her. As Inanna moves closer to the throne, Ereshkigal fixes the "eye of death"[21] upon her and delivers a violent blow, effectively killing Inanna. Ereshkigal then hangs Inanna's corpse on a nail to rot on the wall of the underworld. Clearly, Inanna is now at her weakest and lowest point. But will she rise?

Thank Goddess for the Back-Up Plan

After three days and three nights, Inanna does not return to her temple. The faithful Ninshubur carries out the plan devised by Inanna before leaving. She goes into mourning and prepares a holy lament. She then seeks the help of Enlil, but he refuses her. Enlil reasons that as a goddess with many powers, Inanna knowingly ventured into the land of no return. She must deal with the consequences on her own, he says. Ninshubur then visits Nanna, who responds the same way. Only Enki, her grandfather and the God of Wisdom, comes to her aid.

Moved by compassion, but also pride in his granddaughter's willingness to face the unknown, he takes dirt from his fingernails to create two magical beings—the *kurgarra* and the *galatur*. They are neither male nor female. Enki equips each one with a specific power to alchemically restore Inanna. He connects the *kurgarra* with "the food of life" and the *galatur* with the "water of life." He instructs them to enter the Great Below in the form of flies. Enki knows that Ereshkigal will be playing out the interpenetrating nature of life and death when they find her, symbolically mourning, while enduring simulated labor pains. Her process here underscores the rebirth of both herself and her sister self in the figure of Inanna. Enki instructs his two messengers to mirror Ereshkigal's birth pains by repeating the words of her suffering, thereby appearing to support her with compassion and empathy. Enki knows this kind gesture will elicit a gift from Ereshkigal. He instructs the *kurgarra* and *galatur* to ask for the gift of the "meat" hanging on the wall.

As they arrive, the *kurgarra* and *galatur* find Ereshkigal lying naked with her hair spread out around her in a wild mess, clearly in distress. She is no longer the composed queen of the underworld. Her discomfort overrides her modesty. Moaning in pain, she insists she hurts inside and out. The *kurgarra* and *galatur* meet Ereshkigal in her suffering and mirror her lament.

Astonished at being truly heard with apparent sympathy, Ereshkigal asks: "Who are you,/ Moaning—groaning—sighing with me?"[22] Then, as Enki predicted, she says, "If you are gods, I will bless you,/ If you are mortals, I will give you a gift."[23] Once the *kurgarra* and *galatur* receive Inanna's corpse, they sprinkle the food and water of life on her, and Inanna is instantly resurrected.

THE MYTH EXPLAINED

Sacred Sevens

When Inanna opens herself to the Great Below, she experiences a longing to be reborn. Unknown to her, this is a move toward her initiation into mastery and wholeness. The story begins with a powerful incantation that immediately draws the reader into the experience with its rhythm. The spellbinding incantatory process is every bit intentional. Inanna wants us to learn with her to reap the benefits of her initiation.

As it does throughout her myths, the number seven figures prominently in this story. The seven gates Inanna confronts are the seven levels of initiation in the process of ascension. They relate to the seven chakras, which are connected to the seven notes of the musical octave. Harmonizing their resonance can directly impact our reality. The number seven is also reflected in the seven planetary spheres of the sun, moon, Mercury, Venus,

Mars, Jupiter, and Saturn, offering a cosmological map calling attention to these centers within as a central aspect of our initiation.

Inanna adorns herself with her seven *me*, her earthly possessions. The *me* are also universal laws that govern reality. They are spiritual powers and arts of civilization that support our physical growth and processes. An explanation of Inanna's seven *me* will give us insight into the symbolism and significance of your own gifts and powers.

We can interpret Inanna's crown, or shugurra, as the symbol of her mastery, not only as a leader to her people but also on a spiritual level. Placed upon her seventh chakra, or the crown chakra, it underscores her role as a spiritual teacher. The single strand of lapis beads placed at her neck highlights her capacity to use her voice in a commanding way. These radiant blue beads, positioned to activate her throat chakra, relate to her freedom to speak her truth. Lapis lazuli is a stone believed to promote creative self-expression and communication. The fact that the double strand of beads falls at her breast emphasizes the ways Inanna *nourishes* her people in activating their own clear thoughts and expressions.

The breastplate covering her heart chakra can be seen as an activator of this center of wisdom. It both highlights the heart as well as protects it. All that she has acquired as the Goddess of Love is further enhanced by this breastplate, which broadcasts her heart wisdom. The gold bracelet is a symbol of her wealth and the jewels she has acquired in this life. It is also a symbol of unity, the circle that connects us—a representation of unity consciousness.

The measuring rod and line relate to the ways in which Inanna physically supports her people through surveying the land for its areas of abundance. Similar to the staff of a wizard, the measuring rod and line help Inanna alchemically transmute and create. Finally, Inanna's royal robe is symbolic of her cloak of protection. It is also a part of her majestic beauty.

Its seven pleats convey a significant message about the sacred number seven and the way this number is woven into the tapestry of the initiate's journey.

Inanna must relinquish these seven royal items as she passes through each gate—a profound teaching about letting go of attachment. Each gate presents an opportunity for Inanna and, by connection, the readers of her myths, to examine the corresponding chakra in order to assess any wounding therein, and to bring healing to the area.

Wounding in your chakras can accumulate over time and is connected to your karmic issues. As such, what is built up in your chakras may be lifetimes old. By stripping away an item, Inanna is, in effect, purifying her wounds. She is symbolically releasing whatever had accumulated therein and, as such, is purifying her chakras. This process enlightens us, allowing us to shift toward a higher vibration—the very thing necessary for rebirth.

Every time we deepen our healing, we replace the lower vibrational frequencies that were associated with wounding with the higher vibrations of peace, acceptance, and empowerment. Whenever we surrender to anything, there is an element of faith that is necessary. As Inanna releases her *me*, she surrenders to the laws of the underworld, and demonstrates a faith in herself. Indeed, even stripped naked, she is still equipped with this embodied assurance in herself.

Resurrection As Historical Precedent

Ostensibly, as she tells Neti upon arriving at the underworld, the purpose for Inanna's visit is to attend the funeral of her sister's husband, Gugalanna. In *The Epic of Gilgamesh*,[24] we learn that although it was Gilgamesh who killed Gugalanna, Inanna indirectly had a hand in his death as well by creating a situation in which Gugalanna and Gilgamesh face off. We will explore this further in Gate Seven, but her involvement explains Ereshkigal's anger toward her sister. We can imagine she also envies Inanna's freedom to move about in the great above.

Ereshkigal, now a widow, has been confined to the underworld in darkness, but Inanna possesses the freedom to connect with others and build relationships, to celebrate her sexuality, and to express herself openly. As her sister, Ereshkigal can also be seen as an aspect of Inanna's own self, with whom she has lost touch.

Ereshkigal hangs Inanna, crucified on a nail, like Christ. Significantly, she is granted resurrection after three days and three nights. This noteworthy timeframe becomes perpetuated in later archetypal myths of descent and rebirth, including Christ's own death and resurrection. These details highlight how influential goddess culture has been on Christianity.

Two of Inanna's father figures refuse to help her, demonstrating their own fear of confronting the inner realms and the Death Mysteries. But Enki's role in Inanna's resurrection connects her with the power of alchemy. Enki is a master of magic and known for his alchemical powers. Transmutation is a necessary part of resurrection or ascension. Because he is an alchemist, Enki's role here signifies that we possess all we need to transform into beings of higher vibration who can ultimately transcend. In addition, when Enki creates the *kurgarra* and *galatur* to help free Inanna, he mirrors and thereby showcases the power of his granddaughter's liminality.

The *kurgarra* and *galatur* are sexless beings who defy definition, and like Inanna herself, they embody the liminal. This is significant and highlights a message about resurrection, including all transformations which renew us; we must move beyond limitation to get there. Because the *kurgarra* and *galatur* transcend binaries, they are the perfect beings to negotiate the space between life and death. Equipped with the food of life and the water of life, they represent matter and spirit, respectively. Enki tells them to enter the underworld as flies. As insects that hover near the dead, these seemingly inconsequential beings live between the worlds and are actually restorers of life, underscoring the sacredness of all beings.

The flies are told to emulate Ereshkigal's labor pains when they find her. This is a known therapeutic practice. In clinical settings, we hold space for our clients to express their pain, to sit in that space together, and mirror back their process. It is as if Enki is prescribing the very healing interventions we use as psychotherapists today. As Inanna's sister-self, Ereshkigal's labor pains connect her to Inanna's rebirth. She is also grieving the death of her husband, highlighting the circle of life, death, and rebirth that are all aspects of transition; one begets the other. When the flies repeat Ereshkigal's suffering back to her, she is finally encouraged to have compassion for herself.

In Inanna's journey, she had to let go of her attachments and fully surrender in order to transform, but she also had to accept her process and have faith in the journey. This is a central tenet in freeing the self from the cycle of karma. Even if her hand in Gugalanna's death was indirect, Inanna needed to reconcile the karmic debt of that experience. She does this by entering the underworld herself.

She begins by stating her wish to attend Gugalanna's funeral, but instead attends her own as she is put to death by his widow. She does not simply sit in the world above, taking no action to redeem her mistake. Instead, even if unconsciously at first, she purifies her negative action of indirectly harming him by honoring the dead with her visit and taking on suffering herself. Even Inanna, Queen of Heaven and Earth, is not immune to the law of karma. She innately knows her role in Gugalana's death needs to be balanced, and she tackles it through facing her own shadow.

Ultimately, Inanna's descent teaches us that through courage; the willingness to go through one's initiation with faith and acceptance; the release of attachments; and compassion, we, too, can symbolically resurrect ourselves to become whole.

INTERSECTION: UNDERSTANDING OUR OWN CHALLENGES THROUGH THE GODDESS OF LOVE

Inanna's Call to Spirit: Countering a Loss of Faith

Anyone who has experienced their own version of a descent certainly knows how awful it can feel. The experience often leads to an erosion of faith, causing us to question everything. This can lead us to lose hope as our trust in ourselves and Source—or God, Goddess, the All That Is, whatever term resonates most for you—dissolves before our eyes. When we lose hope, we can begin to leak power energetically, literally becoming disempowered. Do you suddenly doubt everything you once held as true? Does your situation feel unfair and like a cruel act by the Cosmos? From that place of abjection, it is crucial to look for ways in which the experience is aligned with your highest good.

Seeing your trials as an initiation can help. Although this perspective is challenging when you are right in the middle of it, doing so is empowering. Finding a deeper meaning in the experience can reconnect you with faith. This kind of existential crisis or dark night of the soul may present as any number of challenging experiences or recurrent themes in your life such as betrayal, public shame, being called crazy, being blamed for hurting others, being scapegoated, having your truths or creative expressions taken or claimed by another, experiencing body image struggles or an eating disorder, addiction, unrequited love or loss of love, death of a loved one, financial challenges, or generally not being able to make ends meet. It may present as a traumatic diagnosis or an inability to conceive.

It is common to feel as though every ounce of stability has disappeared. You may feel like you are free-falling into the great abyss. When you encounter these types of experiences, seeing them as "gates" in your initiatory process can help you negotiate them with greater ease and grace.

The call to Spirit is when you cast your eyes up from the depths where you have fallen, or actively approached, to understand and feel bolstered by the more profound meaning you can discern. In so doing, you transcend the pain. This call to Spirt often sets in motion an entire paradigm shift that leads to a spiritual awakening and totally alters our reality.

Adopting an Initiate's Mindset

Sure, you may be thinking, this sounds good in theory, but how do you actually adopt the mindset of an initiate? Well, for starters, if you are reading this book, you are someone who longs to understand the truth and to engage in the adventure of life as a way to evolve your soul. You can imagine yourself like Inanna, who embraces the challenge of her descent and gets comfortable with the uncomfortable.

Hold the intention that you, too, will go through your own metamorphosis and be born anew, progressively equipped as you emerge with new awareness into the laws of being and reality. Call upon Inanna to guide you. With her resurrection, Inanna is even more powerful and knowledgeable. She becomes a fully initiated high priestess—a conqueror of the underworld. She is here to help you through the same journey.

This type of journey into the underworld can feel like your life has fallen apart, and yet it may be precisely what is needed most to heal what has been keeping you from living fully in the now. Let us turn our attention to ways you can transcend your own analogous obstacle, so it becomes a strength.

Minding Our Memories: Understanding and Clearing our Chakras

The process of remembering begins with a decision. Let yourself go there. Have you always felt like you are here to do something special and to leave an impact? Could this be the process through which, like Inanna, you step into your wholeness? Symbolically, initiation is the experience of remembering your true purpose.

At this point, it is worth acknowledging the notion of harmonic resonance as it relates to the seven gates and the chakras. Inanna's descent illustrates that her own transformation impacts the whole, as we will see in Gate Seven, where she eventually ascends. The phenomenon of harmonic resonance is woven into the tapestry of the universe. It is about the relationship between entities. What is done to one directly affects the other. Therefore, when you reconcile your karma and move toward liberation, it has an impact on the world at large.

In the myth, Inanna's removal of a garment at each gate is an act of releasing that which is no longer in harmony with the self—a release of attachments that we often acquire on the physical plane. This emotional or mental release shifts the vibrational resonance of the corresponding chakra and can be seen as a teaching she is offering about ascension. In purifying our energy centers and raising our own vibration, we too can ready ourselves for ascension. The higher our energetic vibration, the easier it is for us to align with Spirit and move beyond the attachments of the physical world toward spiritual liberation.

Because chakras contain memory, when we interface with these various chakras through our own process, past-life memories may surface. Some of what is being released, therefore, might not even be from this lifetime. Allow yourself to remember your soul's mission through exploring the feelings and memories that emerge as you encounter each gate. This process will allow you to access greater balance and wholeness. Clearing our chakras so that each one vibrates at the frequency intended aligns us with Source. This shift in our own frequency is always a necessary step in our ascension process. When Inanna passes through the seven gates and lets go of what she was holding onto, the outdated aspects of her die away, allowing her to resurrect—to be reborn into wholeness.

The initiation process includes clearing these energy centers and releasing the attachments therein. In some cases, that will mean the release of potential trauma stored in the body from many lifetimes. Whatever pushback you may have received for being who you are—an agent of change—and doing what you do, in this or other lifetimes, you now have the opportunity to release it.

While it might feel challenging to clear the wounds that have long been stored within, it helps to relate to it as coming up to come out, rather than coming up to re-injure. You must prepare yourself not to get caught in the pull of the emotional pain as it makes its way up and through you. Instead, bear witness to it as a gift of grace.

For example, imagine you are clearing a long-held fear of getting into trouble for doing something wrong. Perhaps in a past life, you were one of the many individuals who were considered a witch or heretic and endured persecution for it. Today, you find yourself in a situation at work wherein you forgot to do something that was expected, and you are reprimanded. It is simply a gentle reprimand, but you feel it so intensely that there is a sensation in your stomach of being gripped by fear. In this scenario, your felt experience far exceeds the actual situation. See it for what it is, an opportunity to meet your long-held fear with the grace of understanding so you can find your footing, recalibrate, and begin to release it.

This process will not necessarily happen in a neat and sequential order from the first chakra to the seventh. Think about each gate we encounter in your descent as corresponding to a chakra in need of balancing. Go to the appendix in the back of the book and explore the chakra chart to see which chakra requires attention. You will have a felt sense of recognition upon reading about each, and it will help you understand the relationship between your own process and the corresponding chakra.

In the course of our journey together, I will illustrate how each of Inanna's myths relates to a particular chakra in each chapter. However, this is meant as a template to help guide your own process. Everyone will have their own individual experience with it, and each gate will refer to your individually corresponding chakra. Imagine your healing process as a breaking up of old scar tissue which gives you access to greater freedom to stretch into who you have come here to be. In the physical body, when scar tissue in muscle is reduced, the area has more flexibility and can move with more ease. In the process of your healing, awakening, and initiation, you may start at the top layer of the symbolic scar tissue and progress toward the bottom layer.

The process of transformation is unique to you. But it will become easier as you go. The initial breaking up of scar tissue, which can be conceptualized as your defense mechanisms, is often the most uncomfortable. Again, this is not a linear process, but the entry point is located where the most work needs to be done. It is not for the faint of heart. To succeed, you need to find your most courageous, unapologetic nature. What is so compelling about this paradigm is how each healing begets a deeper one beneath it, as the thick scar tissue gradually dissolves.

While some of us may have more injury than others in certain centers, this framework encourages a holistic and thorough transformation.

How Do I Know It's an Initiation?

Holding the perspective of our own life as a heroine's journey can embolden our resolve to process the work that needs to be done. It begins with embarkation, picks up speed and intensity as we navigate the journey, and follows its flow into a return. There are helpers and guides along the way and, ultimately, it is about an inner learning. The journey leads us to finally see for ourselves how powerful, courageous, and masterful we are. The journey itself affords this understanding, allowing us to remember who we really are. This is our initiation.

Let us now explore the ways we might arrive at this healing. The spiritual interventions outlined here are geared toward the specific chakras Inanna works through as she confronts each individual gate. Your own process might follow a different order, but working through and balancing all seven chakras will be necessary. By making these connections clear, you will be able to correlate your own experiences as they intersect with each corresponding chakra. Reorient the sequence as it feels right to you.

In this first myth, Inanna's call to Spirit is related to the seventh chakra, the crown. The crown chakra is the connection with one's higher self and Source. Spiritual challenges such as a lack of faith or trust in oneself or Source often appear in the seventh chakra. The call to Spirit helps you develop the ability to have faith in yourself and to be in connection with the Divine, so you may walk a life aligned with your true purpose.

Faith is like a passcode, a vibration that unlocks the connection to Source. Faith not only keeps hope alive, but it helps you feel empowered and grants you access to the strength to move through your process with grace. Let Inanna be your inspiration and allow her to help initiate you into your own power. You are beginning to remember your own Divinity and connect to yourself as the sacred being you are.

Keep your heart open to the emerging transformation by engaging in these practices. When you consciously choose to work with Inanna, you will experience shifts in your life. Get ready, have courage and faith, and embrace your journey back to wholeness.

HEALING INTERVENTION

When you have gone through your own descent and have been forced to give up some your symbolic earthly possessions, such as stability or abundance, initially you might feel disconnected from joy. You might even find yourself resentful of what you have had to let go of. But remember, a call to Spirit is connected to the seventh chakra and is an invitation to develop faith. If you have gone, or are going, through your own descent, have faith that this journey is in service of your highest good.

Let faith also help dissolve resentment, which is the most significant barrier to joy. So, we must begin the process of restoring faith to transmute this negative emotion. Inanna's descent to the Great Below was a choice she made. Importantly, as you will see in Gate Seven, she does not harbor resentment for what she loses or for the challenge she goes through. Instead, she finds a way to turn her experience into a strength that supports the All.

Faith grants you access to a larger perspective, which allows you entry into the state of acceptance. Acceptance is an understanding that all things you encounter ultimately support your evolution, even if it takes a while for you to get there. Sometimes even traumatic experiences can inform our path and guide us toward who we really are by helping us see the strength, power, and resiliency that lies within us.

Spirit Summons: Preparing Your Ritual

Having faith in your process, your descent—your unique journey to the underworld—dissolves resistance and allows acceptance. Get really honest with yourself. Are there aspects of your descent in which you feel unsupported, alone, abandoned? Do you blame yourself for your seeming inability to heal, or for allowing this situation to continue to take up space in your heart and mind? If so, then it is time to release these feelings and allow faith to help you come into acceptance. A lack of faith can make your process far more challenging by making it easier to get caught up in the suffering.

Like attracts like. Lower energy frequency attracts and aligns with lower energy frequency. Conversely, faith restores your inner strength, bolstering you so you are less susceptible to the suffering that can accompany change. We have all experienced some version of a loss of faith in our lives, and the feeling can stay with us for a long time. This is an area where ritual is very useful. The ritual below is a simple but powerful way to reconnect you with faith that will empower you.

Ritual and ceremony are incredibly effective methods for taking inventory of what is in your heart and ready to be upgraded. These sacred tools allow you to make conscious what may be unconsciously influencing your life in a way that may no longer align with you. By using ritual, you become your own healer, your own therapist. Ritual can be advantageous in delivering quick and lasting results. It places the individual in the driver's seat, allowing access to the ability to transform yourself in the here and now.

There are many ways to participate in ritual. Some rituals are elaborate, conducted to create the sacred space to alchemize, such as vows meant to sanctify the union of marriage. Others are less obvious but still set the conditions to cultivate a desired outcome. For example, you might engage in a morning exercise routine to achieve a state of clarity and balance.

To begin your own ritual, call upon your gift of imagination and envision yourself engaging in the art of ceremony, in any form from the past, honoring that which resonates for you. If you feel a particular and compelling recognition upon reading about rituals, you may have used these practices regularly in a past life. There is no right or wrong way to perform a ritual. It is all about intention. Intention is the most powerful aspect of spiritual practice.

Times when the veils between the worlds are thinnest are particularly opportune for ritual. During the eight high holidays in the calendar year, the portals between the higher realms and our own world are more open. These include the fall and spring equinoxes; the winter and summer solstices; and the significant dates of November 1, February 2, May 1, and August 1. But full moons and new moons are powerful times as well. Your own birthday and the anniversary of a loved one's transition can also be powerful. Any time is a good time.

Creating an altar is also a useful way to stay in contact with the Goddess, the Divine Mother, the sacred feminine, and any other high-level beings—like Inanna—to whom you are drawn. Altars offer a sacred bridge between the body and spirit.

You can create an altar anywhere in your home and place on it whatever resonates in your heart. Ask your heart and your own Divine team to instruct you as to what you might want to include on your altar. Your Divine team may include Inanna, your guides, angels, or any higher-dimensional beings.

Altars need not occupy a large space and can even have multiple purposes. Your altar can be designed on the top of a bookcase or chest. You can place anything on it that moves you: stones, crystals, candles, a small dish for offerings—your gifts to the Divine such as sage or sweetgrass—and pictures or statues of a being or deity with whom you feel connected. You might include images of loved ones or a talisman of significance.

Some people include representations of the four elements on their altar, such as a candle for fire, incense or a feather for air, a chalice for water, and a small bowl of sand or a plant or fresh flower to represent the Earth. You do not need an altar to perform a ritual, but it can be a helpful organizing principle.

RITUAL FOR RESTORING FAITH

Items required: A quiet space where you can be alone; a candle; a sage bundle or smudge stick; and a crystal that represents a clearing stone to you.

You can create an altar or an altar-like space inside or outside. This may even be a straightforward circle on the ground. Whether or not you are including a representation of the four elements of earth, air, fire, or water, consciously bring in the fifth element of Spirit by bringing your own Spirit of openheartedness into this ceremony.

Call in the power of the seven directions, starting with the east, then the south, west, north, below, center and above in this order. This can be repeated at the beginning of every ritual, if the process resonates with you. Repeat the following prayer three times:

> May Inanna assist me in accessing faith on every level, so I
> accept my process and feel supported, protected, and guided.
> May she help me heal my seventh chakra.

STEP 1. Now that you have settled into your quiet space, take a seat and close your eyes. Imagine yourself walking through a beautiful archway that leads to a corridor. This corridor is lit with candles hanging from the walls on both sides. As you walk down the corridor you feel yourself bathed in the light of the candles. You come to a staircase, which you descend. There are seven stairs and with each step feel yourself getting closer to your own spiritual core. The last step leads you to a strong sense of grounded safety. You have arrived at the level of your spiritual core.

STEP 2. Notice that there is a fire burning in the middle of the room you have just stepped into, with pillows on the ground around the fire. You take a seat on one of the pillows and invite in your sacred guides. This includes Inanna, and all the beings that you wish to be present to support you with this ritual. Watch them arrive, one by one, and take seats around the circle. As soon as all have arrived, ask for their Divine assistance in restoring your faith so you may access a deep, conscious acceptance of your present situation.

STEP 3. With these allies present in your sacred circle, call up the situation, person, or experience in which you have lost faith. Please note that for some people, the process of recalling such an event can be re-traumatizing. If this is the case, simply speak a brief description of the situation aloud such as "the death of my mother." Your felt sense of safety is of the utmost importance, so ensure you take care of yourself and engage with this exercise *only* at the level that maintains this felt sense of safety.

If you do feel safe calling up the experience, notice if you feel resentment about it that leads to a felt sense of disconnection from Source. See the situation clearly in your mind's eye. Hold it and allow yourself to feel the emotion that accompanies it. With this feeling of discomfort present, open your eyes and light the candle. As you light it, say aloud: As I light this candle, I enable its flame to transmute anything blocking my faith into the vibration of acceptance.

Bring your awareness to the flame itself. Watch it and let it carry you. Be right in the space of the flame and only the flame while allowing the feelings of resentment to be present as your gaze rests upon the light. Take a few moments to observe the flame and allow it to take you wherever it takes you. You have aligned your consciousness with the wish to transform anything eroding your faith. The flame serves as the portal to this process.

While inside the flame, simply observe. Do images appear? Is the flame growing or shrinking? Is it moving, dancing, swaying, or is it fixed? Ask the beings you have called in for this ritual if there are any messages the transmuting flame has for you. Take in those messages. Absorb the transforming energy of the element of fire. Merge with its energy.

STEP 4. Close your eyes now and address the beings you called in for support while positioning your left hand over your heart and placing your right hand, palm outward at your side. Say the following aloud:

Please [insert name of the being you called on; for example, Inanna], I ask that you Divinely assist me in extracting all cords of attachment that connect me to [state the situation, experience, or person] now and from the roots. Please burn these cords with their roots in St. Germaine's[25] violet flame of ascension, to be transmuted into pure, pink, loving light and poured into the Earth, to help the Earth to heal. Please fill in the holes where the roots were within me and within all who are connected to this situation. Fill in theses holes with universal healing energy, emerald green light, gold light, and the highest vibration of love so we are all perfectly whole and pure.

STEP 5. Take the sage or smudge stick and light it with the candle flame. Encircle your whole body with the smoke. Put out the smudge stick. Lie down next to the candle and take the crystal that you have chosen and place it on the ground just above the top of your head at your seventh chakra. Allow your consciousness to come into your crown chakra and the crystal next to it. Feel it. Now ask the being you have called in to assist you in connecting you with the energy of faith. State out loud: I am connected, supported, guided, and held. I embody faith on every level.

STEP 6. While still lying down, bring both hands to your heart and call forth the spacious, open state of faith and acceptance. Out loud, ask the following of your higher self:

> Please make conscious a deep understanding of the ways in which this experience or person has helped me to evolve. Allow me to see with perfect clarity the direct process by which this (traumatic) experience has allowed me to see who I am and the power I possess. Please help me gain access to this understanding now so that I have unconditional faith in myself and Source.

Allow your higher self to speak to you. You may receive insights immediately, but the insights may also come in a few days or through the dream state, so if you do not hear or see anything clearly yet, trust your higher self to find the perfect time and medium to communicate this new information to you. The answers will be revealed and lead you to a genuine acceptance of this situation.

STEP 7. Give thanks to your courageous self for the bravery of this ritual and also to the beings, including Inanna, who joined you in your circle. Lay down some sage from your smudge stick and the crystal you used, in the spot where you were sitting. Leave it there for a few hours to be fully received. Close the ritual by stating:

> I walk in faith, feeling supported on every level. It is so. It is so. It is so.

AND NOW THE REAL STORY BEGINS

Mantra to support process: I am a fully actualized heroine of my own story.

This powerful ritual has set you up to be able to rewrite your story from a place of empowerment. Rewriting your story will help you to see your experience from a truly holistic perspective. Now is the time to evaluate your own life and consider how best you can recast yourself as the heroine you are.

This is one of the gifts that Inanna offers through her own descent. Think about the ways in which you are similar to her. How are you consciously and intentionally engaged with all that shows up in life with courage, confidence, skill, and discernment? What are some of the gates you have encountered, and what emerged as you moved through those?

Prepare yourself to write in your sacred journal about the experience that you would describe as your descent. Before you begin, consider what you feel has completely leveled you, whether you have just been through it or are in the midst of it now. Have you been dealing with chronic illness? Are you grieving the death of a loved one? Have you gone through a divorce or the ending of a significant relationship? Have you lost your job? Are you dealing with an addiction? Does it feel like nothing is working? Do you feel like you have fallen so far out of touch with yourself that you are in the underworld, the dark place of fear, the Great Below?

On page one, title the story, "My Heroine's Journey." Think about the story of your own descent, with you as the heroine who understands her story from the lens of initiation. If your life is your own journey that emulates that of Inanna, how does it follow the theme of the heroine's journey—the departure, the initiation, the return? This descent is a process you are going through that has the capacity to lead you toward empowerment, mastery, meaning, and healing.

Remember that there are always helpers in such a journey. Take a minute to think about who those helpers are in your life. Let yourself see them.

If you have been guided to this book, chances are you have experienced a descent. However, if you have yet to begin yours, this chapter will help prepare you, and you can come back to it with the insights you gain from the following chapters. Allow Inanna's process to provide you with a map of what it might look like and how best to navigate it.

However, if you have already gone through a descent, contextualizing it in very practical terms in your journal can help you make sense of it. Ask yourself the following questions to help position you to reframe the story anew: How did your descent begin? What led to it? What steps did you take to surrender into it? How has it made you feel? Where does this feeling show up in your body? How has your life changed as a result of it? What are the things you had to let go? Do you feel yourself being judged, as Inanna was by the judges of the underworld?

24

While writing, consider how your process has been an initiation, filled with tests to enhance and deepen your skill. Were you forced to give something up? Did you confront self-doubt? What do the next steps look like as you prepare to heal? What is the gift in the process? Once you have explored these questions, note your responses in your journal.

Now go back to page one of your journal and read it aloud, through to the end, to see how you have just transformed your old story into one of empowerment and successfully moved through your own heroine's journey. Congratulations! Celebrate your bravery and willingness to grow. Allow this shift inside to help you hold a wide lens in your life always, to see how everything has a sacred purpose and teaching in this holy curriculum. Let your seventh chakra heal and enable you to have faith in yourself.

By first restoring your faith in yourself, you are poised to perform as the heroine of your own life. Understanding your story as an initiation marks you as brave, courageous, and capable of actualizing your dreams. The ritual supports the faith needed to cast yourself as the unapologetic heroine you are. You will see, as we approach the next gate, how embodying this role permits and promotes further evolution.

You are now ready to go deeper. You have the context to understand your experience and you have brought balancing, clearing, and transformation to your seventh chakra. At the next gate, we will explore healing ancestral relationships and will see how Inanna masters the ability to negotiate generational wounds and transform them. As a heroine, you are capable of this very same level of mastery.

Gate Two

HEALING ANCESTRAL RELATIONSHIPS

THE MYTH

Inanna and the God of Wisdom

We enter this myth as Inanna has grown into her role as the Goddess of Love. In Inanna's lifeline, this myth occurred before her descent into the underworld. Now deeply connected to her generative power, we find the crowned Inanna leaning back against an apple tree, gazing at her exceptional vulva in reverence of herself. In this moment of reflection, she recognizes her full potential and becomes inspired.

She knows that she has just gone through an evolution and is equipped with a new confidence in her role as queen, capable of leading her people using her embodied womb wisdom. Always attuned to her inner guidance, Inanna's contemplative practice of connecting with and honoring her womb acts as a doorway to her origin. She begins to think about her familial lineage and decides to go visit her grandfather, Enki.

Inanna's high priestess magic permeates this story. We see this in the words Inanna utters to herself, manifesting the desires of her heart via prayer: "I shall honor Enki, God of Wisdom in Eridu./ I shall utter a prayer to Enki at the deep sweet waters."[26] Inanna clearly wants something from Enki, even if she is not yet clear what that is. As the God of Wisdom, Enki possesses truths she is ready to receive.

Inanna sets off for Enki's temple. Because Enki is attuned to spiritual energy, he is already preparing for her arrival. He tells his servant Isimud to meet Inanna and welcome her with refreshments and beer at the "holy table." Once Enki arrives, the two begin imbibing heartily and toasting one another.

The two drink more heavily and, as Enki becomes intoxicated, he begins gifting what are called his *me,* which he holds in his possession. The *me* are the spiritual cultures of the land and the laws of civilization. They are the attributes which help people connect and allow a civilization to flourish. Enki's *me* include the ability to develop intimacy with others, a deep appreciation for wise elders, musical instruments and song, the ability to make decisions, the ability to soothe the heart, the capacity for straightforwardness and counseling, and a prioritization of heart-centered joy. Enki gives these *me* to Inanna, saying:

> In the name of my power! In the name of my holy shrine!
> To my [grand] daughter Inanna I shall give
> The high priesthood! Godship!
> The noble, enduring crown! The throne of kingship![27]

Enki toasts Inanna each time he gifts her with more *me*, which he does fourteen times. Naturally, wise Inanna willingly accepts, declaring as she toasts him back, "I take them!"[28] He drunkenly offers her all he has, including the capacity to descend and ascend from the Great Below, forthright speech, the art of sexual intercourse and foreplay, the art of the hero, and the art of power and kindness. He also gifts her the ability to perceive deceit, to travel safely, and to use the tavern as a location to effectively organize and build community among her people. Inanna accepts it all and takes inventory of her gifts one by one, loading them into her boat. Enki is so drunk that he asks his servant to help ensure Inanna gets to her city of Uruk safely.

Upon Sober Second Thought

Once he has sobered up, Enki looks about his holy temple and sees that all his *me* are gone. He asks Isimud what happened, and Isimud recounts the events of the previous night. Deeply remorseful for having fallen under the seduction of the goddess, he tells Isimud to unleash his frightening creatures to retrieve Inanna's boat and all the *me*.

Isimud goes to Inanna and explains that Enki wants the *me* returned, but that she herself can continue on to her city. Appalled at Enki going back on his word, which she experiences as an act of betrayal, Inanna becomes enraged. When the creatures try to take her boat, Inanna sets loose her mighty servant Ninshubur on them, who we already know is both devoted to Inanna and capable of mastering the gods.

With a "slice" of the air, Ninshubur vigorously pushes the creatures back to their home, retrieving the boat. Enki tries five more times to reclaim his gifts, using different frightening beings, from giants and sea monsters to the "watchmen of the Iturungal Canal."[29] Each time, Ninshubur is successful in fending them off and protecting her queen.

Inanna Succeeds and Enters Flow

Ninshubur advises Inanna to let the water flow into the city as they approach her temple. Inanna then commands "the high water to sweep over the streets."[30] The boat of Heaven docks and for the seventh time (the sacred number seven again), Enki asks Isimud where Inanna is and finds that Inanna has arrived in her city of Uruk.

However, this final time, it seems Enki has changed his tune and has returned to a place of acceptance and open heartedness. He acknowledges that Inanna has caught the attention of her people as she docks her boat full of power. He wants to witness this moment, and he hurries to Uruk himself.

As she arrives in her boat, Inanna can sense the awe-inspired wonder of her people. She then begins to unload the *me*, offering them generously to her people. As she unpacks each *me,* she identifies it for the crowd. Something interesting occurs in this scene. The *me* have multiplied—there are more now than originally gifted to her by Enki. This emphasizes how the act of giving proliferates. These new offerings include the art of women, which is the feminine knowledge and understanding of sensuality and passionate love, and the ability to use the *me* perfectly.

Enki then appears, no longer trying to retrieve the *me,* and joins Inanna to endorse her generosity. He blesses her city and her people, declaring, "Let the city of Uruk be restored to its great place."[31]

THE MYTH EXPLAINED

In the first part of the story, Inanna celebrates her "holy vulva," underscoring her acknowledgment and appreciation of her second chakra with its capacity to create and cultivate. This celebration of her holy vulva as an applauding of self can be seen as a ritual that allows Inanna to get in touch with, and to conjure, her capacity to manifest what her heart desires. She is connecting with her feminine magic. This is obviously something she feels she needs in order to heal her ancestral line.

During Enki's inebriation, he gifts to her all the attributes and powers she consciously or unconsciously came for. Even while she engages with him in consuming the beer, Inanna does not lose her senses. She stays sober, her oracular gifts informing her that something significant is about to happen. Ultimately, by presenting her with his gifts of *me*, Enki is actualizing a transfer of power.

Her Water Breaks: The Rebirth of Her People

Ninshubur is Inanna's servant and guide, but she also represents Inanna's higher self, the part of her that is already actualized and devoted to her enlightenment. When Ninshubur fights off the creatures unleashed by Enki, we see the aspect of Inanna that is resolved, fierce, focused, and driven. There is no way she is giving up this opportunity—these are her *me* now, to do with as she envisions. It is her destiny to share them with her people and to bring to them the wisdom, gifts, and power that will help them go through their own evolutionary processes. She wants to help lift the consciousness of her people.

When Ninshubur proclaims "Let the high water flow in our city,"[32] causing the streets to flood, she is enabling Inanna to dock gracefully at her home and to make a grand entrance. It is also a way in which Inanna extends the historical trope of the great flood and the subsequent renovation of civilization, reminding us of her role in and commitment to helping uplift humanity. She declares, "Let the little children laugh and sing./ Let all of Uruk be festive!" [33]

Enki gives Inanna the sacred culture of the land, which she immediately brings to her people. But Inanna gives Enki something formidable in return. She acts as a catalyst for him to deepen his own healing process and, as such, she restores her ancestral line. The exchange is reciprocally beneficial. By attempting to repeal his generous offering of the *me,* Enki highlights his fear about his identity without them. As the receiver of his gifts, Inanna helps Enki to understand that the sacred laws and the power we gain through evolution (the *me*) must be shared, and not retained possessively for one's own self-aggrandizement. In turn, Enki helps Inanna emerge as a sacred guide to her people, a leader worthy of their praises. Indeed, the two transform each other, becoming both student and teacher to one another.

At the end of the myth, Inanna receives even more *me,* specifically, the art of women and the ability to use all the *me* perfectly. By staying committed to this healing of her ancestral line and subsequently sharing the gifts she receives with her people, as the devoted leader she is, Inanna gains even greater access to her potent feminine magic. Receiving "the art of women" at the end of the myth confirms Inanna as a sacred guide of feminine consciousness—a master of unconditional love, compassion, unity, and heart-centered wisdom.

INTERSECTION: UNDERSTANDING OUR OWN CHALLENGES THROUGH THE GODDESS OF LOVE

Inanna's Process of Healing Ancestral Relationships

We get a deep look into the dynamic of Inanna's family line in this story, and it is profoundly relatable. Inanna demonstrates how to access and embody one's dominant ancestral strengths while also healing ancestral wounds and refusing to take them on.

In the meeting between Enki and Inanna at the "holy table," we witness Enki get completely intoxicated and do something that he later regrets. How many of us have witnessed a family member do this at a family function? Even though he changes his mind afterwards and goes through a process of regret before he finally fully releases the *me* to Inanna, his ultimate act of generosity is a gesture many of us never get to experience from family members.

The modeling here is important. It highlights that we can, indeed, inherit positive familial attributes through healing our ancestral line. Additionally, the content of the gifts is significant. Symbolically, the *me* represent what we inherit in the way of skills and strengths from our family line.

When his heart finally swells with generosity, Enki gifts Inanna all the tools a culture needs to evolve.

Confronting the Dark Side

Perhaps the altered state of his inebriation allows Enki to drop a protective barrier, during which he sees how much good Inanna can bring to her people through his gifts. However, when he sobers up, limiting fears—surrounding his own identity without the *me*—return. This struggle with power used for self-aggrandizement is played out as he retaliates, sending six different intimidating beings to his granddaughter's boat to retrieve the *me.*

Metaphorically, the creatures can be seen as the psychological wounds and limiting tendencies that we may inherit from our ancestors. As the creatures try to overwhelm and disempower her, Inanna resists. She remains steadfast and engages the resource available to her: the magic of her faithful servant and guide, Ninshubur.

Ultimately, Inanna is committed to her self-realization as a supreme leader, insisting: "Let the lands proclaim my noble name."[34]

She recognizes this is part of her destiny and insists on manifesting it. She knows the time has come to fully inhabit her role as a Divine leader and to use her gifts to uplift her people. By enacting this faith in herself, Inanna rises above the affronts of her grandfather, who initially showers her with gifts, then betrays her with the use of violent force.

The intimidating creatures Enki unleashes on Inanna signify the threads of violence that can be present in our ancestral line, originating from the misuse of power. These were Enki's unhealed wounds and, ultimately, Inanna was a catalyst for him to reconcile these wounds.

Inanna knows that the *me* must be shared and cannot be held on to. She understands that what we learn, acquire, and cultivate is best expressed as something we give back to humanity, through walking a path of compassionate service. The fact that Enki comes full circle so quickly is a testament to the efficacy of Inanna as a teacher. She knows that like herself, at his core, Enki is committed to the uplifting of humanity. This was her original inspiration at the beginning of the myth.

After ritualistically conjuring her generative potency as she leaned against the apple tree, meditating on her holy vulva, Inanna thinks of Enki. She realizes in that moment that he is the only member of her family constellation who can provide access to the strengths and truths that will enable her to lead and uplift her people. She is, after all, a high priestess, a seer, and an alchemist in her own right. She listens to and follows the intuitive guidance of her own heart.

We Are More than Our Wounding

Further exploration of Inanna's family system reveals trauma in her lineage. In the myth of *Enlil and Ninlil: The Begetting of Nanna,*[35] we learn that Inanna's other grandfather, Enlil, raped her grandmother, Ninlil, resulting in the birth of Inanna's father, Nanna. As a result of this violent act, he is banished from his city to the underworld.[36] By contrast, Inanna's mother was born from a loving connection between Enki and Ningikuga.

Trauma has the capacity to impact our relationship with self. Such a profound violation as rape can impact generations beyond the original victim. Despite this very painful trauma, Inanna reigns supreme as a role model for a healthy, vibrant second chakra of creativity and sexuality. We see no trace of this specific generational trauma in Inanna, who is known as the Goddess of Sex and reveres her vulva. Instead, we see her significant strength and fortitude, and her confidence and wholeness regarding her second chakra.

Inanna demonstrates to us that we need not be defined by our traumas and instead can come to embody the strength of working through them. Energy follows focus; when we bring consciousness to positivity, we raise our vibration. Even if she feels a pull to her wounds, Inanna chooses to focus on what is in harmony instead of what is out of tune. It is a process of empowerment. Similarly, as therapists, we support and highlight the strengths of the individual to bolster what needs healing and restoration.

How do these strengths and wounds show up in your own lineage? Do you see the gifts from your family system that you wish to carry forward and perpetuate? Has there been a misuse of power somewhere in your ancestral line? Are there erroneous beliefs influencing the family perspective, such as a belief around scarcity? Are there spoken or unspoken rules governing your line, such as a "rule" that demonstrating emotions or allowing yourself to be vulnerable is a weakness?

Consider your own ancestral relationships and decide what you would like to keep and what you would like to heal. Below, we explore how to take on only what is aligned with your highest good.

HEALING INTERVENTION

The healing of ancestral relationships is associated with the throat chakra. This chakra is connected with finding your true voice. Balancing this chakra allows you to have the ability to speak your genuine truth—one that incorporates the strengths and gifts from your ancestral line—without taking on the lower vibrational frequencies of unhealed wounds. In healing the throat chakra, you ensure that your story is fundamentally your own and is free of generational wounds.

Preparation for Ritual

The following ritual allows us to bring consciousness to experiences we have inherited and to assess whether those resonate with where we are currently. Oftentimes, we unconsciously perpetuate inherited patterns or behaviors that aren't serving us. In other cases, there are things left unsaid or business left unfinished with our family members. Now is the time to give those parts of us the opportunity to be heard and seen.

Begin by sitting in a quiet space with your back straight. Avoid reclining, as sitting up straight will engage the conscious mind rather than the unconscious aspects of self. This is different from the reclined position of traditional psychoanalysis, which facilitates access to the unconscious. Here, we are addressing and actively engaging conscious material in order to transmute, heal, and empower ourselves.

With eyes closed but staying alert, do a quick body scan. Follow your whole body in your mind's eye from the ground up, noticing where you may be holding tension. Breathe into that space to break it up, and ready yourself to access a flexible emotional attitude for this exercise.

Upon completion of the body scan, ask yourself what aspects of your own ancestral line need to be worked through and healed. Let the situation or individual come into your conscious mind.

Perhaps you have a family system wherein your primary caregiver was emotionally unavailable due to their own wounding. As such, they were unable to bestow upon you the love you needed so that you could feel whole. Was there abuse present, or a tendency to keep things hidden or unspoken? Did addiction surface and create a breakdown or lead to shame? Maybe there was a betrayal that occurred which created a chasm in the family system or elicited feelings of guilt or blame. Perhaps an illness or death led to fear, grief, pain, or even feelings of abandonment. Now is the time to give voice to that impactful experience and let yourself release what is not yours to carry.

To understand this in your own life, consider what messages are governing your family system that may no longer resonate for you. What beliefs or narratives would you like to release? You can go further with this exploration by writing in your journal about what comes up. Take the time you need to explore these patterns within yourself. Once you have completed this step and you have identified what you want to release and what you wish to keep, then you are ready for the following ritual.

FULL MOON ANCESTOR RITUAL

Do this ritual on a full moon, alone or with folks who may be accompanying you in your pursuit of liberation and self-acceptance.

Items required: A few pieces of paper, a pen, altar, a pitcher of water, a red crayon or red paint, a piece of cloth, a blanket upon which to sit, some form of offering like a dried flower or sage, and a few small items like shiny buttons or small stones that you have found that speak to you and that represent beauty. If you live near the beach, seashells or sea glass also make great offerings. Choose something that feels special enough to be used in your prayer bundle.

Go to a spot outside at night under the full moon, ideally out in nature. If you live in an urban setting, find a park, or even just sit beside an open window where you can see the moon. Speak the following prayer:

> May Inanna bless and heal my generational line and help me
> to bring forth the gifts of my ancestors.

STEP 1. Take a seat and close your eyes. Imagine the full moon shining above you, and feel her celestial light shower down over your seated self, engulfing you in a radiant moonbeam. Imagine her light penetrating even the spot upon which you sit, anchoring you into the Earth while also protecting you.

STEP 2. With your eyes closed, call out to Inanna and all the moon goddesses who have historically been worshiped. Ask them to come to you to deliver guidance and moon magic. You can be specific and call them by name, if you know of them directly, or you can simply state: I call in the moon goddesses with whom I have been historically connected throughout my lifetimes to support me in this ritual. These, too, are your ancestors.

Ask for their Divine assistance in releasing what you are ready to let go of and in calling in that which you are now primed to bring forth in this present moment. Finally, call in your specific ancestors—your familial line—and ask them to also be present to support you in transmuting what is ready to be healed in you and on their behalf.

STEP 3. Sitting on the ground, remember what you have already identified in preparation for this ritual, and write up a list of inheritances from your family line that you are ready to release—the outdated patterns, tendencies, scripts, or behaviors that no longer serve you. Once complete, write up a list of strengths and gifts from your family line that you want to call in now and make manifest in this moment.

STEP 4. Take the list of what you are ready to let go of from your familial line and use your red crayon or red paint to color over the entire list so that every word is covered. Take the pitcher of water and pour the water over this now red paper, a symbol relating to the purification and release of the feminine cycle.

STEP 5. Take the list of the gifts and strengths of your ancestors that you are ready to receive and read them aloud in your own strong and powerful voice. Speak to the moon and all the beings you have called in to join you in your sacred circle. As you read your list aloud, know that you are calling the list into being. Wrap the list in the piece of cloth, along with the small items of offering that represent beauty in your eyes.

Place this prayer bundle either outside under the moon for the night or on a windowsill in your home, exposed to the moonlight. After the night, place the prayer bundle on your altar until the next full moon, allowing the strengths and gifts of your ancestors to be honored and celebrated for an entire moon cycle.

STEP 6. Know in your heart that it is finished. State aloud: Everything intended in this ritual has been fully accomplished in all directions of time and space.

STEP 7. Quietly say a prayer of gratitude to yourself, Inanna, the moon goddesses, and your ancestors who showed up to support you.

Example of a list of what you may wish to release:

> I fully release and let go of all anxiety, stress, worry, insecurity, self-doubt, fear, and anything blocking me from actualizing my highest potential that I may have inherited from my ancestral line. I let go of anything blocking my ability to be in a fulfilling relationship, anything blocking perfect physical health, anything blocking my creative process, and all that is not mine to carry. I release these all fully now and in all directions of time.

Gate Two: Healing and Ancestral Relationships

Example of a list of what you may wish to call in and bring forth in this now moment:

> I make manifest all the strengths, wisdom, gifts, talents, and power of my ancestral line. I am supported by my loved ones on every level and all my ancestral relationships are healed now. I remember fully who I am and what I have come here to do, and I walk my destiny with great ease and joy. I reconcile all aspects of myself, including my right and left hemispheres of the brain and my masculine and feminine expressions. I anchor in, fully receive, and embody all of these: health, balance, strength, love, calm, joy, physical fitness, play, passion, patience, lightheartedness, equanimity, sexual pleasure, and creativity. I call forth all gifts, skills, and wisdom that I have acquired from my ancestors and in all my lifetimes to help me serve the Light now. I and all those whom I love are fully protected, joyful, peaceful, and blessed with abundance and fulfillment on every level. I am free and embody the love, power, and strength of my ancestors.

Commit to this ceremony for at least three and up to thirteen lunar cycles. It will help you to keep the list of things you have asked to show up, because in one month, when you are ready to do the ritual again, you will be able to see what you have manifested on the list. It will be fulfilling for you to see just how powerful you are.

High Frequency Vibrations

The full moon ritual allowed you to bring healing to your ancestral lineage, to ensure you are vibrating at the highest frequency possible. Think of it as a deep cleanse for the soul, a way to align you with harmony. Ultimately, it is a way to own your voice. This full moon ritual is a process that helps expand and balance the throat chakra so you can speak your truth, infused with strengths and gifts from your ancestral line instead of the wounds you also might have inherited. The process supports you in using your powerful voice with authority to give back what is not yours to carry, and to proclaim your readiness to perpetuate only that which is aligned with your highest good. This has prepared you for the step that comes next.

In Gate Three, we will explore moving beyond addictions, which is about releasing attachments. You will need a clear, strong voice to declare your readiness to proceed. Call on Inanna to accompany you in working through addictive patterns. She will use her powerful and holy ammunition to help you liberate yourself.

Gate Three

MOVING BEYOND ADDICTION

THE MYTH

The Huluppu-Tree

The story of *The Huluppu-Tree* begins with an explanation of how Heaven and Earth, originally unified as the Cosmic Mountain, were separated. The world came into being as the god An carried off Heaven and the god Enlil carried off Earth, thereby establishing two separate domains.

The Goddess Ereshkigal is forcibly assigned to preside over the underworld. Enki, the God of Wisdom, unsuccessfully attempts to rescue Ereshkigal from this fate, but the underworld rises up and turns against him in the guise of a storm, devastating his boat and halting his efforts.

The tale then turns abruptly to the natural world and specifically to the description of a tree:

> At that time, a tree, a single tree, a huluppu-tree
> Was planted by the banks of the Euphrates.
> The tree was nurtured by the waters of the Euphrates,
> The whirling South Wind arose, pulling at its roots
> And ripping at its branches
> Until the waters of the Euphrates carried it away.[37]

The huluppu-tree comes into being and the amniotic fluid of the Euphrates helps to nourish and support the sapling. When the wind uproots it, the nourishing maternal energy of the river carries the tree to the feet of Inanna, who was then just a young girl walking by the river. Always attuned to her destiny, Inanna pulls the tree from the river and declares that she will take it back to her garden. She replants it, firmly packing the earth around it with her foot to ensure it takes root. She cares for it, hoping that one day it will grow large enough to provide her with the wood for a throne and bed. As she grows, both her longing and the tree grow with her.

After ten years, Inanna intuits her readiness to receive her throne and bed. Excited to step into all they represent, she approaches her tree. However, she is horrified to discover that frightening beings have taken up residence in her beloved tree. There is "[a] serpent who could not be charmed" coiled about its roots, an "*Anzu*-bird" and his young have made a nest in its branches, and the "maid Lilith" has built her home in the tree's trunk. Inanna is devastated and begins to weep. Despite the goddess's tears, the beings refuse to leave.

Not knowing what to do, Inanna goes to her twin brother, Utu the Sun God, for help. Utu rises, marking daybreak. Inanna recounts her story of finding the tree at the dawn of creation in the waters of the Euphrates, retrieving it, planting it in her garden, and nurturing it over many years. She explains that fierce, unwanted beings have taken up home in her precious tree. She needs help removing them so she can use the tree to build her throne and bed, using the wood that she has been waiting years for the tree to yield.

Her throne and bed in this story symbolize her queendom and sexuality. Utu refuses to help her. The next day at dawn, she goes to another brother figure, Gilgamesh, the same warrior who killed Ereshkigal's husband Gugalanna. As she did with Utu, she recounts her tale. As a warrior hero, Gilgamesh accepts the challenge.

Donning the garments of his warrior power, Gilgamesh reaches for his heavy bronze ax as if it were light as air. Gilgamesh knows he is meant to help Inanna, and he goes to her garden. He approaches the tree and strikes the snake, causing the bird and his young to flee and making the maid Lilith irate. This is the very Lilith that we see later in the Bible. In her rage, she destroys her home in the tree's trunk. Gilgamesh uproots the tree, and his attendants cut off its branches. From what remains, Gilgamesh carves Inanna's throne and bed.

In return, Inanna uses the roots and the upper branches of the crown of the tree to create two gifts called a *pukku* and a *mikku*; one is a rod-like object and the other is circular like a ring.[38] These gifts mark Gilgamesh as a hero for his people.

THE MYTH EXPLAINED

There is a distinct cadence to this tale about Genesis. Its use of rhythm evokes the controlled, undulating breath of a mother in labor and emphasizes the process of bringing forth. Representative of every woman,

Inanna comes of age and into her power in this story. As such, it is her own creation myth as well as that of the world. It is also a story that captures the activation of the heroine archetype. She stands alongside the hero Gilgamesh, foreshadowing her own role as heroine.

In the beginning of the story, we find Inanna in her youth. She is a young girl longing for her future as a queen and the power that comes with this role. In addition, she is yearning for her sexuality—her sense of herself as a woman. To achieve that, however, Inanna must free herself from the three beings inhabiting her tree and impeding her progress. She must actively remove these beings in order to actualize her goal of using the tree for what she wants. Wise and humble enough to know that she needs help doing so, Inanna reaches out to her brother figures, figuratively balancing masculine and feminine energies to do so.

The story identifies a feminine process of becoming that centralizes the merging of masculine and feminine forces within us. As we saw in the introduction, "Freefall: Finding your Bearings," this practice of inner and outer union was unique to goddess cultures. Feminine energy was sacred in the goddess cultures, but it was not meant to dominate masculine energy; rather, it was meant to exist alongside and in connection with the sacred masculine. Such a stance elicits peace within and without. Here, we see Inanna coming of age and learning the need for internal balance in order to fully embody her power.

We can imagine the three beings symbolize the inner shadow aspects to which Inanna is attached. She must release them to activate her potential. The beings in Inanna's tree are representative of addictive thought patterns and behaviors to which the mind can become unconsciously tethered. Such negative patterns must first be made conscious to be reconciled. Letting them go gives Inanna access to what she craves: the freedom to own her sexuality, power, and sovereignty.

Our Fears Made Manifest

Let us now explore the significance of the beings who take up residence in Inanna's tree: the snake, the Anzu bird, and Lilith. From a psychological perspective, the snake can be seen as the sacred sexual knowledge that Inanna fears she won't be able to control. Like the kundalini coiled about the base of the spine at the root chakra, the snake is coiled in the roots of the tree.

Kundalini is the serpentine energy that moves up the spine through the chakras. When an individual learns how to work with it, the potency of the kundalini can awaken the third eye and lead to enlightenment. The presence of the snake, therefore, can be seen as Inanna's unconscious fears and anxieties about her ability to handle her own kundalini power and whether that power will be accepted in the world.

In *The Myth of Anzu*,[39] the Anzu bird—who is part lion and part eagle—is granted the role of protecting the Tablets of Destiny. However, he attempts to steal them for himself so that he may have power over all, including the gods. For Inanna, the presence of the Anzu may signal the way that she, too, will have to negotiate her relationship to power as a queen. The Anzu illustrates the potential for the seduction of power, forcing Inanna to examine if she has what it takes to rule while aligned with the highest good and avoid the temptation to misuse her authority.

Lilith, originally called Lilitu in Sumerian mythology, is a night demoness. At times, she is portrayed as a succubus who resides in desolate places and takes the form of a human woman to seduce men through sex. Other stories depict her drinking the blood of children and torturing sleeping men. Later, she appears in Hebrew myths as Adam's first wife, who refuses to lay beneath him, believing herself equal to him. When Adam disagrees, Lilith leaves the Garden of Eden in pursuit of her independence.

Lilith, then, may signify Inanna's own resistance to being tamed or confined by heterosexual conventions—the part of her that longs for sexual connection and yet does not want to be bound by anything.

The presence of Lilith highlights Inanna's cognitive dissonance as she negotiates the external expectations of her role as queen alongside her king, while knowing her true nature is polyamorous. Lilith is associated with an insatiable sexual appetite. Inanna may fear that she will not be satiated, and that her innate tendency to pursue whatever she wants may conflict with her requirements as queen. Inanna does not conform just because it is expected of her; Lilith represents her fear of being misunderstood as she follows her own path.

Looking for Brotherly Love

To help move beyond her addictive patterns—as exemplified by the snake, the Anzu bird, and Lilith—Inanna seeks support from her brother figures. She approaches the Sun God, Utu, at dawn, just as he begins to rise, symbolizing a readiness within her—an awakening. For anyone who has struggled with addiction, there are moments in which we feel particularly emboldened in our resolve to conquer those patterns. Often this occurs at the beginning of the day, before the daily stresses of life have begun to creep in.

When Utu refuses, we see that it is not just any aspect of the masculine that is required, but the skillset of a hero. Inanna needs someone to match the activation of her heroine archetype. Ultimately, it is Gilgamesh who accepts the challenge, and a process unfolds between the two. They join forces, balancing the polarity of the masculine and feminine.

Gilgamesh is invited to help Inanna move deeper into her womanhood. Simultaneously, Inanna's request for help elicits the opportunity for

Gilgamesh to more fully embody his manhood. As the instigator for this process, Inanna becomes the teacher, guide, and inspiration for his journey toward enlightenment.

The Sacred Tree of Life

Gilgamesh also acts as a catalyst for Inanna to connect with her inner courage. Whereas Utu represents the wounded or reluctant male, incapable of the courage required to support and collaborate with the feminine represented by his sister, Gilgamesh willingly accepts the challenge. Among the many rich and multidimensional meanings of this story, here again we are reminded of the importance of reconciling the shadow aspects of self, as seen in Inanna's wounds and fears, as well as balancing the masculine and feminine within.

Gilgamesh enters Inanna's garden and reaches first for the snake, metaphorically activating the kundalini power as he delivers his blow. Activating the kundalini can elicit a *kundalini awakening* as it rises up the spine. If it successfully does so, passing through each chakra and ultimately activating the third eye, it expands to the crown chakra and merges with Source.

This myth is not just a story of Genesis, but a guide for the return to Heaven, from which the Earth separated at the beginning of the story.

Centrally, the prioritization of a woman as the protagonist of the story who ultimately masters the Tree of Life is antithetical to many myths propagated by male-dominated religions. Inanna's is a myth of the Divine Feminine. Here, not only does Inanna master the Tree of Life, connecting the axis between Heaven and Earth, but her wisdom and capacity to comprehend the truth and seize her destiny are expressly articulated and celebrated.

Many scholars have noted that the Tree of Life is a map for our ascension that also resides in the body.[40] It aligns with the spinal column, with the kundalini serpent coiled at the root chakra. The autonomic nervous system connected to the spine is made up of the sympathetic and parasympathetic nervous system. In addition, we have the right and left hemispheres of the brain and the energy of yin and yang within us. The balancing of these polarities is associated with successfully mastering the Tree of Life within ourselves.

The myth of *Inanna and the Huluppu Tree*, therefore, instructs our spiritual evolution. The symbols of the snake and Tree of Life have long been connected to the Divine Feminine. The Canaanite Goddess Asherah, for example, herself a high priestess of sacred sexuality, was celebrated and worshipped through the erection of Asherah poles—potent symbols of the Tree of Life, which were carved and erected like statues to honor her.

The Egyptian goddess Isis is also connected to the Tree of Life through her association with the acacia tree. For the Egyptians, the acacia tree contained the power of both life and death and was related to magic and healing.

An Exchange of Gifts

Even as a young girl walking by the river, Inanna was able to discern the significance of this sacred tree, highlighting her gift of prophecy. Ultimately, Inanna knows her power is connected to the symbolism of the serpent who could not be charmed—the kundalini energy. As the Goddess of Love and sexual love, it is essential that Inanna let go of her attachment to her fear of kundalini energy so that it may serve her as intended. She has to overcome her ambivalence in the face of its power so that she can share what it has to teach us.

Inanna's process of clearing the tree of its intruders enables her to actualize her destiny as the Goddess of Love and the Queen of Heaven and Earth. Just as in Gate One, where Inanna was forced to let go of her earthly possessions and move beyond attachment, here, Inanna's initiation grants her access to her path as a teacher of ascension.

In exchange for the gifts of her "shining" throne and bed—her queendom and womanhood—Inanna gives Gilgamesh a *pukku* and *mikku*. The meaning of these specific items is not yet clear. Samuel Noah Kramer suggests they may be a drum and drumstick.[41] Others have proposed they might have been part of a game, like a ball and stick resembling the sport of field hockey.[42] Importantly, however, their reciprocity comes to the foreground as Inanna helps Gilgamesh play out his role as hero. This symbolic balancing of Divine Masculine and Divine Feminine consciousness is necessary to move up the Tree of Life. Living on the physical plane, with all its sensual feedback, creates a risk of becoming overly attached to behaviors—patterns of thinking, feelings, and beliefs—that might become addictions. By moving beyond those attachments, we gain greater access to our Divinity.

INTERSECTION: UNDERSTANDING OUR OWN CHALLENGES THROUGH THE GODDESS OF LOVE

Inanna Moves Beyond Addiction

This myth, like Inanna herself, is multifaceted. Ultimately, it can be read as a story of releasing attachments and overcoming addictive patterns, both of which are directly linked to our capacity to reach enlightenment. The three beings who take up residence in Inanna's huluppu-tree symbolize the roots of her addictions—her unhealed wounds. They also represent the embodiment of various expressions of addiction to power. The Anzu-bird belies his charge as protector in an attempt to dominate all, even the gods. The snake—historically a symbol of knowledge—embodies the potential of using knowledge gleaned through the wisdom of the kundalini to dominate others. Lilith may represent the addiction to one's own carnal appetites, particularly in versions of her where she is rendered as a succubus who takes energy from others to feel empowered.

The Origin of Addictive Behaviors May Be Purposefully Protective

What is at the heart of addiction? Why do some of us struggle with such a challenge, while others seem impervious to it? Inanna needed to release herself from her attachment to unresolved fears, drives, and urges in order to live her truth. There is an inner liberation that occurs when we overcome addiction. The root of addictive tendencies is wounding. If left unresolved, primal wounds can fester and hook us through the self-medicated release we seek from them in the haze of our addictive behaviors.

However, these addictive behaviors originally served a purpose, and we should remember that. Our initial connection to the behaviors—whether an addiction to sex, social media, work, shopping, plastic surgery, exercise, food, or even substance abuse—began as a means of self-soothing, even if these activities are now fundamentally unproductive and harmful. Some addictions are more culturally condoned than others, such as an addiction to exercise versus substance abuse. In truth, however, the compulsions are similar. It would serve us to recognize this so that we can transform the stigma associated with many addictions. Stigmas can cause us to feel shame and can complicate recovery. We must bring healing to the wound at the root of addiction in order to begin to feel free.

Addictions are simply any behavioral patterns that you feel *compelled* to engage in. They exist on a spectrum. This spectrum might mean some behaviors are more or less time-consuming or impactful in our lives. Some addictions are very subtle and require you to be extremely savvy in calling these out for yourself. We all have addictions on some level. Be blatantly honest with yourself in identifying what yours might be.

Do you find yourself checking social media to see if something new has popped up in your newsfeed, even though you just checked five minutes ago? Are you anxious to see how many people have "liked" one of your social media posts? Do you get Botox or fillers regularly—but each time feel like you need to do more to get it exactly right? Do you rely on caffeine throughout the day for energy? Do you feel compelled to "hit the gym" even when a day of relaxation and rest might be more productive?

As you can see, some common behaviors that you might not imagine are addictions actually are. You must be willing to acknowledge the behaviors you feel compelled to engage in. They are an invitation to practice letting go.

Less Obvious Aspects of Addiction

Let's examine the hypothetical example of an addiction to food. Imagine that the individual dealing with this addiction began this behavior as a direct result of sexual abuse sustained as a child. The trauma of this violation is the core wound. This person may have felt ashamed and anxious or been forced to keep the violence a secret, thus preventing this individual from getting the support needed and the clinical intervention that would lead to healing and protection from further violation. Feeling unable to speak about it due to the shame, and perhaps pressure by the perpetrator, this person kept it inside and tried to bury it by way of repression.

But the psyche always wants homoeostasis, so it keeps bringing the trauma to light; aspects of the experience break into the conscious mind as flashbacks or anxiety, despite attempts by the individual to repress it. When the trauma surfaces, the increase in fight or flight chemicals from the sympathetic nervous system causes an increase in cortisol, which leads to an increase in serotonin re-uptake. Serotonin is the feel-good neurotransmitter. The individual then feels the brain's signal and it shows up as a craving for that "feel good" hit, which can come from carbohydrates and sugar. In addition, an individual might unconsciously create a shield of protection around themselves through excess weight in an effort to keep them safe from the threat of further violation. The end result shows up as an addiction to food.

Exchange Addiction for Powers of Mastery

You can see from the example above why it is not useful to stigmatize any addiction. Also, you can see how the behaviors might have originally served a purpose. If you are reading this chapter, you have already signaled to your higher self that you are preparing to heal the core wound underlying an addictive pattern. Crucially, you must relate to yourself in this process with compassion, as transformation is not always straightforward or immediate as we would want it to be.

Overcoming addiction equips you with strength we might liken to Inanna's *me*—those spiritual powers and arts of civilization gifted to her by her grandfather, Enki, in the Gate Two. Letting go of attachments, including addiction, is a central precept of spiritual evolution. It raises our frequency and helps us become the most impactful version of ourselves by transcending limitations, raising our frequency, and moving us toward our own mastery.

HEALING INTERVENTION

This challenge of addiction deals with reclaiming our power and thus relates to the third chakra, the solar plexus. This is the center where we process our negative emotions at the root of addictive tendencies. A balanced solar plexus allows you to let go of attachment with more ease. In addition, a healthy third chakra supports your empathic orientation while protecting you from absorbing, through clairsentience, any energy that is not yours to carry. Clairsentience is the ability to perceive intuitively through sensation and is one of the four mediums through which we access our intuition.

Let Go and Let Goddess

There is a saying in 12-Step programs like Alcoholics Anonymous and Narcotics Anonymous that underscores the methodology of success: "Let go and let God." The phrase concretizes the idea of giving our struggles over to a higher power and welcoming in Divine assistance. I invite you to put this concept into practice.

Along this journey, you are remembering your own Divine nature; there are certain aspects of the Goddess that will be uniquely resonant for you. At this point in your own initiation, the Goddess wants to make a personal connection with you. For this to happen, simply ask, while meditating, that you be shown the specific goddess that is most aligned with your soul's purpose. It may be Inanna herself, or Inanna may link you to a goddess that you are meant to work with right now.

In meditation, simply ask: Inanna, please guide me with ease and clarity to the goddess I need to support me in this now moment. Please lead me to discover which goddess I am meant to collaborate with now, so I may remember the ways in which her heart wisdom supports me.

Some of you may get an instant response. Others will be inspired to look up various goddesses over the next few days, perhaps based on areas of geographical interest, signaling a memory of your own connection to that particular country or culture.[43] Are you pulled to the Celtic lands, to Egypt, to the Americas, to the wisdom of the East, or to the brilliance of the native peoples of our Earth? Perhaps your guide is White Buffalo Calf Woman, Isis, Quan Yin, Mary Magdalene, Cerridwen, or Parvati.

Follow the tug of your heart to the connection that shows up. Allow your inner guidance to direct you in this search. Below is a ritual to help you create a formal connection and enter into supportive mentorship. Draw on her energy to help you overcome addiction. "Let go and let goddess!"

RITUAL TO CONNECT WITH THE YOUR TEACHER OF THE HIGHER REALMS

Items required: A quiet space where you can be alone, a candle, and an artist's rendition or the printed-out name of your goddess. Recite the following prayer:

> May Inanna support me in connecting with the energy of
> the goddess I have chosen to help me transmute and release
> any addictive tendencies or patterns I am ready to let go of.

STEP 1. Center yourself and settle into a comfortable position. Close your eyes. Imagine you are sitting in the middle of a beautiful, golden, five-pointed star. Looking at yourself from above, this pentagram extends beyond your physical self to surround your auric field, as well as the whole room in which you are sitting. It protects all aspects of you. Bring your awareness to the seat under you and feel the support of the ground beneath you.

STEP 2. Ask the sacred pentagram to act as a gateway for you to join with the goddess you have chosen.

STEP 3. Place the image of your goddess at eye level across from you. With heart open and eyes closed, ask her to come forward and make herself known. As you do this, gently open your eyes to look at the image and consciously call in the vibration that she emits. Bring your awareness to your crown chakra. Feel her raise her left hand and hold it over your crown, pouring forth all the strength and gifts that she represents as your ally, your soul sister in this journey of remembering who you are and what you came to the Earth plane to do. Feel yourself receive and take in what she is sharing.

STEP 4. Lie down and close your eyes. Place your left hand over your heart and your right hand over your womb. See yourself reclining on the sand of your favorite beach or the soft grass of your favorite green space. The sun is warm. There is a gentle breeze, and you are aware that no one else happens to be in your chosen spot today. While lying there, you hear your name being called. It is a familiar voice. The tone is soothing and softens all resistance, helping to reset your own physical vibration.

You get up from your spot on the sand or the grass and find a small path through the dunes or field. It takes you to a bench looking out at the waves crashing on the shore or the beautiful forest before you. Standing beside the bench is the goddess you have chosen. She motions for you to sit down. She takes a seat to the left of you and takes your left hand in her right hand. She tells you she is grateful to connect with you and asks if you will allow her to help you let go of your addictions and attachments and bring forth her energy into the world.

Sit for a moment to contemplate this question in your heart. Respond in whatever way you are inspired to. Your free will cannot be violated, and it is only by consciously choosing to collaborate in this way that it will occur. Whatever answer you feel moved to give is perfect. She explains that you two are connected in your mission to help uplift humanity and restore balance within and without. She reaches into the garment she is wearing and hands you a small box. You take it and thank her.

You open the box and find a message inscribed on a small gold tablet—a code unique to you to help with your liberation and transformation. You hold this gift to your heart and embrace her. Her gift is now a part of you. It symbolizes her unconditional support of you and bestows upon you the capacity to liberate yourself. With this confirmation, you stand up, knowing that you can bring her to you at any time simply by calling her name.

You walk back down the path in the dunes or grass away from the bench where the goddess stands and watches you with pride. You return to your spot on the beach or greenspace. Lie back down and rest so you can integrate this experience. Take as long you need. When you are ready, slowly bring awareness and energy back into your feet, your toes, your hands. Take a deep breath and slowly sit up, remembering with ease all that transpired. The gift your goddess gave you will assist you as you go forward.

STEP 5. Bring your awareness back to the five-pointed star that is surrounding and protecting you. In your mind's eye, reach out to touch the golden star with your hands in gratitude for its role in this introduction to your goddess. Bow your head to honor all that has transpired and watch the star dissolve into particles of light before your eyes, marking the completion of this ritual.

If you have chosen to let the goddess work through you and support you in your own growth, maintain this connection and nourish it by intentionally asking for her comfort and guidance. For example, you may say: Please, Goddess, clear my energy field with your Divine energy so I may walk freely in alignment with my highest good and make choices that are healthy and support my evolution. Ask her to help you release all addictions and attachments, and to share the wisdom, strength, and courage needed to walk your destiny.

Connect with the message, the unique gift she gave you in the ritual above. Study her, read about her, and spend time accessing her energy so that you can channel the mastery she represents. Allow her energy to support you in the journey of your own evolution.

Commit to regularly and intentionally aligning with this connection for at least a full moon cycle. You may notice at the end of that cycle that she wishes to stay with you. Perhaps at that point she will guide you to another goddess who is seeking to connect with you. You are now linked to the cosmic sisterhood, and as long as your free will is aligned with this connection, it will remain intact. Through your powerful intention and free will, you make it so. Intention secures it into being in the Akashic field, the space which connects us and contains all that is, has been, and will be, and which holds the constantly updated living record of the Cosmos.[44]

How it All Fits Together

The ritual and guided meditation helped you establish a connection with a higher power on whom you can lean and to whom you may hand over the addiction. Overcoming addictive behaviors cannot be done at the urging of someone else. It must come from within. The meditation supports your internal process to call in the higher realms to assist you. Now that you have "let go and let goddess," you have taken the steps internally to shift toward your inner freedom from whatever was previously binding you. Inanna and the goddess you chose to work with both have your back, and you are equipped with all you need to live free from attachments that are no longer serving you. True healing comes from self-acceptance.

In exploring the next gate, we will see how Inanna demonstrates strong self-acceptance and owns her beauty and confidence. Be inspired by Inanna to own your beauty as she does, and believe that you, too, can embody the confidence of a goddess and see yourself through a Divine lens! Self-love is an essential step in our ascension. We must vibrate at the frequency of love on every level.

The next gate takes us through the process of activating love of self.

Gate Four

ACHIEVING POSITIVE BODY IMAGE AND SELF-ESTEEM

THE MYTH

The Courtship of Inanna and Dumuzi

I n this tale, Inanna is a radiant young woman who is not yet fully aware of her majestic presence. The myth begins when Inanna is approached by her brother, the Sun God Utu, who believes it is time for his sister to find a mate. Although their conversation concerns flax and its growth, it is overflowing with sexual innuendo, implying the fecundity of the goddess herself. Utu explains how he, an embodiment of the Sun, will transform the flax into Inanna's "bridal sheet" and help usher in her fate. Persuaded by his explanation, Inanna has no reason to doubt what Utu says and so begins to explore worthy suitors. She asks:

> Brother, after you've brought my bridal sheet to me,
> Who will go to bed with me?
> Utu, who will go to bed with me?[45]

Who Under the Sun Can Match Inanna?

Being the Sun God and one of the seven who can decree fate, Utu can see Inanna's destiny. He encourages Inanna to consider the shepherd Dumuzi as her mate, highlighting that Dumuzi was "conceived on the sacred marriage throne."[46] In her typical fashion, and despite asking for his guidance, Inanna resists this suggestion. She insists that her heart is with another: the farmer she has been fantasizing about. She regards the farmer's capacity to grow and harvest as an indication of his ability to give and receive with respect. Again, the language in this section is rich in innuendo. However, Utu continues to proclaim Dumuzi's attributes, emphasizing: "Whatever he touches shines brightly."[47]

Utu wants Inanna to see Dumuzi's potential. As she begins to feel her body awakening to the pull of sexual desire, Inanna is both excited and cautious. She is not yet exactly sure what she is looking for, so she leans toward what appears overtly fulfilling. The farmer with whom she has been flirting fills her storehouses with grain, and she imagines this means he can do the same sexually. She is not yet aware of the subtle nuances of the female orgasm.

Unconvinced by Utu's urgings toward Dumuzi, Inanna declares that she will not marry the shepherd, for she has not yet seen his ability to be seductive, gentle, or attentive. Instead, she observes, "His clothes are coarse."[48] Suddenly, Dumuzi himself appears and valiantly defends his worth, articulating the many ways in which he is a perfect match for her. In an attempt to showcase his valor over the farmer, Dumuzi lists the offerings he can provide that parallel those of the farmer.

Inanna is still unimpressed. Her lack of understanding of her own erotic desire creates an impasse between the pair. Dumuzi refutes her dismissal by continuing to confidently insist on his impressive worth. Unexpectedly, she stumbles into what she finds attractive; someone who knows what he wants. As Dumuzi fights for her, she gets caught up in a heated debate with him—and the sexual tension builds. Aroused by his unyielding pursuit and the strong case he makes for himself, she starts to find him attractive. She begins to feel something stir inside of her, and Dumuzi begins to shape-shift in front of her eyes as the more worthy choice. Inanna comes to her decision on her own; Dumuzi will be her lover.

The Arousal of a Goddess

With Inanna's choice made, Dumuzi then goes to the royal home bearing gifts, which demonstrates his ability to pay tribute, honor, and have reverence for this spectacular Goddess of Love. At her door, he asks for her to "open the house."[49] Excited by his arrival, we can imagine her rushing to the window to peek outside, seeing him in his glory with his hands full of gifts for her. Her nascent longing has now turned into a fully-fledged lover's desire.

Suddenly, she finds herself enraptured and runs to her mother, Ningal, for guidance. Ningal helps her prepare for her sacred meeting with Dumuzi, including arranging her dowry. Under the guidance of her mother, and in celebration of her own beauty, Inanna dons her royal robe and drapes jewels about her neck.

Dumuzi waits patiently but is full of excitement himself. When she is finally ready and opens her door, Dumuzi is taken aback, smitten by her beauty. Inanna *feels* herself as radiant; "Inside the house she shone before him/ Like the moon."[50]

In the exchange that ensues between the two lovers, Inanna unapologetically declares that her own sexual pleasure is a priority. She contends:

> My vulva, the horn,
> The Boat of Heaven,
> Is full of eagerness like the young moon.
> My untilled land lies fallow.
>
> As for me, Inanna,
> Who will plow my vulva?
> Who will plow my high field?
> Who will plow my wet ground?[51]

The text plainly reveals Inanna's erotic effect on Dumuzi, as in the line: "At the king's lap stood the rising cedar."[52] Inanna, in turn, acknowledges that his burgeoning desire is a result of her power and beauty. She is becoming aware of the impact and potency of her sensuality. This awareness inspires a romantic repartee in pastoral language: "My well stocked garden of the plain," she says to him, "He is lettuce planted by the water."[53] In turn, Dumuzi honors her with, "O Lady, your breast is your field…I will drink all you have to offer."[54] She responds by declaring to Dumuzi that she will guard her sacred womb and protect it.

A Sacred Ritual

Dumuzi asks Inanna to accompany him to his garden. They walk through the trees, stopping at his apple tree, where he explains that he wishes to plant his seed. Inanna kneels before it. The imagery shifts to a symbolic metaphor where the two begin to sing to one another. In song, we see Dumuzi rise out of leaves on the ground while plants pour forth from Inanna's womb. This is a ritual of sorts, in which the two are preparing to consummate their connection. He is preparing for a sexual union with the Goddess of Love, after all. Since she is a queen, everything about this initial act is sacred, holy, and intentional.

Ignited from within, Inanna is ready. The scene shifts to Inanna's royal home where she commands the sacred union, summoning her sexual altar, her holy bed. She pulls the bridal sheet across it herself. She acknowledges her carnal desire to reciprocate. The chemistry between the two is unmistakable.

Dumuzi proves himself a generous lover, earning Inanna's favor and securing his position as her husband. In return, she decrees his fate. Acknowledging that he is fit to take the title of king and provider for her city, Inanna declares he is the chosen one to sit upon the throne and to wear the crown, kingly garments, and holy sandals.

Once Inanna decrees his fate, her guide and counsel, Ninshubur, blesses Dumuzi, asking for him to be granted an honorable reign, wherein the holy union that ensues protects and supports the fertility and abundance of the people and land of Sumer and Akkad[55]. Dumuzi returns to Inanna and they "rejoice," giving in to the impassioned pull between lovers. Afterwards, Inanna reflects on their sacred union and acknowledges that they consummated their love fifty times.

Fulfilled, Dumuzi is ready to go to the palace and tend to his work as king. Inanna concludes with a meditation on the allure and sweetness of her beloved as she releases him to his duties and relishes in her own post-orgasmic bliss.

THE MYTH EXPLAINED

Although this is a story of the blossoming connection between Inanna and her beloved, it also represents the Maiden aspect of the Goddess, as Inanna learns to own her connection to her body and sexuality. The Maiden is part of the triple moon in which, from waxing to full to waning, the three aspects of the of the Goddess are represented. This trinity includes the Maiden, the Mother, and the Crone. In the Maiden stage, Inanna comes to see herself and her radiance clearly. She comes to understand her sensuality and the importance of entering into a sexual partnership that resonates with her.

Significantly, it is her brother Utu who reveals to Inanna her readiness to consider romantic love. Being the Sun God, Utu is symbolic of the Divine Masculine activating the Divine Feminine. As explored in Gate Three, balancing the Divine Masculine and Divine Feminine—and the parasympathetic and sympathetic nervous systems—supports the process of these two currents moving up the spine, which is the main branch of the central nervous system. This represents a full activation of all three and is associated with mastering the Tree of Life.

As the Goddess of Love, Inanna's connection to her sensuality is central to who she is and all that she brings to her people. With the ability to decree fate, Utu identifies Dumuzi and his regal lineage. He suggests that because Dumuzi was conceived in sacred marriage, he is therefore a worthy match for Inanna. As an independent thinker, however, Inanna must arrive at her own decisions. Initially, she refutes her brother's foresight, insisting that the farmer has the capacity to fill the symbolic storehouses, as she says, of her sacred womb center.

Inanna Considers Her Options

In comparing the farmer and Dumuzi, Inanna notes that Dumuzi's clothes are rough, in keeping with his rough or direct personality—an attribute she shares with him. As she hears herself describe Dumuzi to her brother, she begins to notice, to her surprise, how similar they actually are.

When Dumuzi himself enters the scene, Inanna sees even more clearly how aligned they are. Like her, he is driven, determined, and courageous. He stands before the Queen of Heaven and Earth and proclaims his worth as her lover. This self-assured confidence is incredibly attractive to Inanna, and it mirrors her own. The fact that Dumuzi knows what he wants excites her. As this recognition unfolds, Dumuzi transforms in her eyes, becoming her destined beloved.

It was necessary, however, that Inanna come to this realization herself. It was not sufficient simply to be told of it by her brother. Inanna must *feel* the choices she makes. Deeply attuned to her body, Inanna uses it like a pendulum—a tool to access what resonates and what does not. As she and Dumuzi begin to engage in conversation, Inanna begins to feel her connectedness to him, confirming for her that he is her beloved.

Inanna's emphasis on her own body as a source of wisdom and guidance highlights the potency of clairsentience, a medium through which we can access our intuition. Clairsentience connects us to Spirit through feeling, often referred to as a "gut feeling."

With Heart Racing

Once she has made her decision, Dumuzi arrives at Inanna's house bearing gifts of milk and cream; these are gifts that will benefit her people and the land. Much like the Divine Mother who can nourish all with her milk, here we see Dumuzi's capacity to bring nourishment to her people. This represents how Dumuzi will be able to provide as the Divine Masculine. Inanna understands that his contribution enhances her and her world. As her confirmation of their connection grows, she experiences the sensations and excitement of new love.

Having engaged the Divine Masculine through Utu's initial activation, and then through her sensual ignition with Dumuzi, Inanna goes to her mother, Ningal, for guidance around how to prepare for sexual union. Here we see the potency of womb wisdom passed on through the maternal line. Ultimately, it is the Divine Feminine, her mother—the moon goddess, Ningal—who acts as a guide to enable Inanna to activate her sexual prowess.

Once she opens her door to Dumuzi, she details her longing and her body's readiness to have her vulva "plowed." Inanna's explicit request that her sexual needs be met is vastly different from the idea of submissive sex, in which fulfillment of the other is prioritized. To make such a request is to acknowledge one's own longing and to prioritize one's own pleasure. Central to this section of the myth is that Inanna's voice sanctions, for an entire culture, the message of honoring one's own sexual needs as a woman.

Inanna's Holy Vulva

In the Sumerian culture, honoring female sexuality was a central topic of cultural myths long buried, safely evading the destruction that much of the culture sustained. Even today, Inanna reminds us how powerful it is for a woman to embrace her sexuality and prioritize her own pleasure. This is central to reclaiming her power.

The myths of Inanna came about in an era before the Church maligned the sacred sexuality of women. Thanks to the ancient mythographers of the Near East, we have these potent stories to remind us of the way it was—an invitation to women of today to celebrate themselves unapologetically.

Additionally, the poetic exchange between Dumuzi and Inanna highlights the sexual act as natural and inspiring, thereby diffusing the element of shame around sex for the modern reader—a shame initiated by the Church. By contrast, sexuality in the myth is represented as something worthy of celebration.

> My caresser of the soft thighs,
> He is the one my womb loves best,
> He is lettuce planted by the water.[56]

Here, Inanna's cultural perspective of openness, comfort, and ease around sex cultivates respect for and a sense of comfort with one's own body. She proclaims to Dumuzi that she will, with her Divine power, guard her "sheepfold" and watch over his "storehouse." She is referencing her womb, literally and figuratively calling her sexual organ the "shining quivering place which delights Sumer."[57] Inanna is the protector here, an empowered embodiment of the feminine. She is confident in her ability to ensure the safety of herself and her beloved.

Ritual Preparations

As Dumuzi and Inanna walk through his garden, he stops at his apple tree. Significantly, this impactful scene predates the story of Adam and Eve from the Book of Genesis, which contemporary biblical scholars now believe was written between 500 BCE and 400 BCE.[58] Symbolic of the Divine Feminine, apples are associated with vibrant health and eternal life. Apples, then, are the fruit connected with the capacity of the Goddess to grant life and take it away. The Crone aspect of the Goddess knows that death is not an end, but that life is eternal, so the life she takes away is a rebirth.

Here, Inanna kneels at the foot of the apple tree. In a fantastical shift in the scene, we see an homage to the fertility rites that later become part of their sacred union. Dumuzi rises up from the leaves on the ground and comes toward Inanna. Plants then pour forth from Inanna's womb, including grain. This magical scene captures Inanna's commanding power to summon her love from the Earth to meet her glory. It is also a foreshadowing of her descent story, her journey into the Great Below, wherein she dies, is reborn, and becomes her ultimate expression of self, the Queen of Heaven and Earth as well as the underworld—the complete goddess.

Significantly, the process of Dumuzi rising up from the dead leaves at Inanna's feet marks her as intricately connected to his rebirth. Here she is a guide for ascension. The story of her descent and subsequent ascent sets the stage for a lengthy New Year's celebration in Sumer of Divine consummation that is intended to bring fertility and abundance to the land.

Dumuzi felt it necessary to take her to his garden, saying, "I would go with you to my apple tree,"[59] establishing the apple tree as an altar at which to kneel and ritualize the sacred act that is to come.

On the Terms of a Goddess

Ultimately, it is Inanna herself who spreads the bridal sheet across her own bed. She is the one taking charge. The consummation unfolds according to her timeline and her readiness, and she commands it. Being the Goddess of Love, Inanna has a healthy sexual appetite and a strong endurance. They make love fifty times. Notably, she decrees Dumuzi's fate, declaring him fit to sit upon the throne and rule alongside her. And it is through sexual union with her as High Priestess and Queen that he is sanctified and anointed officially as her king.

INTERSECTION: UNDERSTANDING OUR OWN CHALLENGES THROUGH THE GODDESS OF LOVE

Inanna's Positive Body Image and Self-Esteem

In this myth, Inanna emerges as a powerful representation of positive body image and self-esteem, as well as an embodied example of a woman who knows what she deserves. Her process of coming into herself and connecting with her sacred sexuality is instructive for young women within our own culture. Given our historical past and current socio-cultural messaging, many women develop imbalanced relationships with their bodies. They grow up feeling separated from their bodies, with dysmorphic perspectives of their own temples. Many girls and women today are not just ambivalent about their connection to their bodies but are even self-abusive. Let Inanna demonstrate how to honor the body with respect and intention, specifically around sexuality.

Understanding Our Collective Dysmorphia

Issues involving body image and self-esteem often have their root in the second chakra. To be sure, there is a collective injury sustained therein under historical patriarchal dominance, which, even from past lives can merge with any trauma and violation of this creative center that we have experienced in this current life.

Body image and self-esteem were areas of specialization in my clinical psychotherapeutic practice. Very often, trauma was at the root of challenges in these areas, causing feelings of being tainted and undeserving. As we explored in the introduction "Freefall: Finding Your Bearings," there was an overt attempt on the part of the patriarchy to vilify and decimate the mystical power and sacred magic of the feminine second chakra. Many of us have also endured actual trauma in this center in this lifetime, which can cause us to disconnect from our sexuality, creativity, felt sense of safety, and our self-worth.

The unresolved injury might manifest as guilt around nourishing the body that had been dishonored or shamed. This can result in anxieties around what we believe we deserve and ambivalence about sexuality and womanhood. Such conditions can prompt us to develop the skills of running and numbing, including destructive behaviors such as eating disorders, exercise addiction, or even self-harm.

The End of a Cycle

Even within sports culture, many female athletes are erroneously taught that some or all the aspects of the Female Athlete Triad are normal and simply part of competing and training. This pervasive syndrome has many long-term physiological symptoms. What is known as the Female Athlete Triad consists of disordered eating, amenorrhea, and thinning of the bones, resulting in stress fractures due to osteopenia or osteoporosis. The lowering of body fat is often desirable in sports, not only as an aesthetic ideal, but also incorrectly believed to be ideal for performance. The less weight to carry around the track, to haul up the balance bars, to pirouette through the air, the better. In order to achieve this ideal, however, athletes engage in many harmful practices, which are ignored or even encouraged by coaches. Therefore, such abuses become normalized.

The quest to pursue an excessively lean body is manifested through disordered eating, which can include extreme dieting, cutting out entire food groups, rigid calorie control or bulimia, a cycle of binging and purging, and overtraining. The latter is a practice of pushing the body through extreme and rigorous workouts in hopes of whittling down. Such behaviors can result in amenorrhea. Unconsciously, this hormonal imbalance might be an attempt to dry up one's powerful womanhood to avoid the patriarchal wounding that has long been connected to it.

These behaviors often lead us to seek help and, as such, call us to address and heal the internalized guilt that is often at the root of an ambivalent relationship with body and food. Those who suffer from this might have internalized the cultural oppression of women's physicality, making it hard for us to feel justified in nourishing ourselves appropriately. We might feel guilty taking up space in the world—causing us to hide behind layers of protective weight or whittle away, becoming amenorrhoeic and eliminating life-force blood. All may be a reaction to a fear of the patriarchal response to feminine power.

Inanna Teaches That the Body is a Temple

The path of Inanna is intricately aligned with the body. Lars Muhl notes in *The O Manuscript*, his exploration of the Divine Feminine, "The body must be satisfied just like the spirit. The merging of body and spirit is the realization of the perfect human being for a woman."[60] The body itself is a temple, a doorway to connection with Source. This path of living unapologetically is an opportunity to reconfigure our relationship, as women, to the physical, and to move beyond the ambivalent relationships we may have with our own bodies.

To be sure, the patriarchal influence of our culture and the messaging of social media project false images of perfection. These images further cultivate a problematic relationship to self. Daily, we are bombarded with expectations of how we "should" look. It is no wonder so many of us have distorted perspectives of our own bodies and feel disconnected from them.

A Note About Inanna's Trauma

It is important here to address another myth called *Inana* [sic] *and Shukaletuda.*[61] In this myth, Inanna emerges as the teacher we have come to know, offering wisdom and an empowered perspective as well as liberation from woundedness. It highlights her role as a goddess who brings about justice, an attribute she shares with her twin brother Utu. This story also accentuates a strong second chakra when Inanna refuses to identify as a victim after sexual assault.

In the myth, she sets out to survey the land for injustice and wrongdoing. With the dedication of an athlete, Inanna goes up to the mountains and circles Heaven and Earth for perspective, committing to this pursuit until fatigued. Weary, she lies down by the roots of a poplar tree to sleep at night.

A mortal gardener named Shukaletuda is tilling the land nearby. The myth depicts him as incompetent, detailing his inability as a gardener. He takes notice of the goddess from afar. Seeing her asleep in all her glory, he goes to her. While the goddess is deep in slumber, he violates her. He then leaves and tries to hide, realizing she will avenge him. Indeed, when she awakes, through inspecting her sacred vulva, she realizes what has happened and vows to find her perpetrator and ensure that justice prevails.

Furious, she first commands blood to fill the wells throughout her land. Then she conjures a windstorm, a flood, and a dust storm. Finally, she blocks all travel by shutting down the roads—but still she cannot find him. Ultimately, she goes to Enki to seek counsel and demand justice. He agrees, and commands it into being.

Inanna then turns herself into a rainbow and stretches across the land to be sure she can track the perpetrator from every angle. Shukaletuda makes himself as diminutive as possible, but Inanna finds him. He recounts to her what occurred and admits his crime. She condemns him, and justice is served.

But instead of holding on to resentment, Inanna decides to rise above her own hurt. She shifts her experience of violation by ending his perpetrator consciousness. She accomplishes this by declaring that his name will become immortalized and turned into song, alchemizing the energy of his act into a higher vibration through art.

This decision also alters victim consciousness and changes it into empowerment consciousness. Inanna refuses to be bound by trauma and instead uses her power to convert the violation into a teaching for all her people—the songs of Shukaletuda echoing through generations. These songs become both a warning and a medium through which to heal and access the grace of higher consciousness.

Inanna embodies the strength to ensure justice for herself and also to teach us how to transcend acts of violence done against us.

Relate to Self Through Your Sacred Womb

The *vesica piscis*, a symbol long associated with the deeper, hidden teachings of Christian belief systems, is the almond shape of the intersection of two overlapping circles. It represents the merger of the Divine Masculine and Divine Feminine to create the Divine Child, the new way, but it also represents the female sexual organ. It highlights that, as women, we possess the portal to higher consciousness since all of creation was born from the sacred womb and had to pass through the female sexual organ, the doorway of the vulva, to come into physical life.

When we reclaim this powerful truth, we can begin to reconfigure our relationship with our bodies. We rise above the destructive cultural messaging and inhabit our bodies as a source of strength and as the Divine vehicles they are for our glorious spirits. There are many means of doing this, including yoga, dance, active or movement meditation, and also techniques that access the body through quantum healing.

When you begin to remember the truth of who you are on this path, you are invited to begin to clear and heal the trauma held in the body. This healing then enables a more productive relationship with the temple that houses the Goddess, as she is embodied on the Earth plane through each one of us. Doing so can adjust our gaze in the mirror so that we may perceive our true beauty.

Stop Feeling Guilty

As mentioned, the impact of historical wounding on our second chakra often shows up as a feeling of guilt, which we might consider the internalized oppressor. Indeed, moving through guilt and beginning to dismantle it can bring to light how pervasive internalized oppression is. Those who are driven to connect with truth and unity consciousness, and who pursue spiritual evolution, are often met with persecution and attempts to mute or halt their efforts.

After many lifetimes of this kind of experience, the negative messaging the subjugator has used against us has a way of becoming internalized through our worn-down energetic boundaries and defense mechanisms. We then find ourselves echoing the voice of the oppressor to ourselves in the manifestation of our own guilt.

By reframing guilt, we can transform a challenging lived experience into an experience of conscious and deliberate dismantling of the internalized oppressor. In so doing, we are able to show others how to do it as well. However, this highlights an especially important point; we must always start with the self. We must come into congruence ourselves to be authentically capable of accessing our power to heal fully and bring about positive change for and with others.

How Do You Treat Your Temple?

Let Inanna help you cultivate your sacred connection with your body. As a representation of the Goddess, how you treat yourself matters. Do you honor your body as a temple to the Goddess? Do you speak to yourself with the language of love? Do you share your body only with partners of the highest vibration—those willing to act in reverence to you?

As the Maiden aspect of the Goddess, Inanna's relationship with her sexuality is for her own fulfillment—not to become pregnant, but for the experience of pleasure. That is why iconography of Inanna often depicts her with one foot resting on a lion, insinuating her will to direct her own pleasure. This is a reference to the sexual position of being on top and her knowledge of how to maximize clitoral stimulation. Inanna insists on satisfying her own pleasure. It is important for women today to be reminded of the prioritizing of positionality. Inanna represents that, in the beginning, a woman's pleasure was paramount.

In addition, Inanna celebrates beauty. Historically, Inanna's worshippers would drape themselves in jewels and don makeup for her ceremonies to honor both her and their own bodies as sensual and sensualizing.[62] It was part of their magical rites. When you hold this level of sacred connection to your own power and adorn yourself as a goddess, symbolically or literally, your partner merges with that sacred intention as you become a conduit.

Your partner then cannot help but be moved into a higher state of consciousness just by virtue of the relationship you create with yourself. This exchange is powerfully erotic. Allowing your own sense of power, sacred beauty, and sexuality to be arousing, in and of itself, heightens your ability to surrender.

HEALING INTERVENTION

Body image and self-esteem are linked to the second chakra, also called the sacral chakra. It is the energy center of satiating appetites and nourishing self and, as such, is directly connected to your relationship to your body and your self-esteem. It is also the center wherein we give ourselves permission to experience joy.

Blood Moon Meditation for Restoring the Second Chakra

In this meditation we are calling on the power of a Full Blood Moon, during the time of a Total Lunar Eclipse. We are conjuring its transformative energy to transmute and heal any lingering injury sustained from the subjugation of feminine consciousness throughout history. Allow it to help heal all wounds connected to this creative center so it may be fully restored.

Let yourself relax and be healed with ease. If you have a moonstone crystal, use it for this meditation. Alternatively, any crystal can be used. You also can do this meditation without the use of any crystal.

Find a comfortable space in which to recline for about fifteen minutes. If using a crystal, lie down and place the moonstone (or any other) crystal on your second chakra. Now position your left hand over this crystal and your right hand over your heart and imagine healing, golden light pouring into both centers. State the following prayer three times:

> May Inanna help me to heal, balance, restore, and fully activate my second chakra.

Meditation Guidelines

Lie down in a comfortable position and close your eyes. Imagine yourself under a Blood Moon/ Lunar Eclipse on the shores of a beach. Allow the energy of your imagined surroundings to bring you peace.

Bring your attention and your awareness to your sacral chakra at your sex organs, below your belly button. Wherever you are, feel the connection to Mother Earth through the ground beneath you. She is supporting you upon her altar where you are lying, and the lunar eclipse is showering you with positive energy from above.

Allow all stress, all worry, all concern to drain from your cells right into Mother Earth. She has the capacity to transmute that energy into pure, loving light and to recycle it to nourish the planet. Release all energy that is not serving you.

Take a few deep breaths now, exhaling fully to encourage and make space for relaxation, calm, and tranquility. There is nowhere else you need to be right now. Allow yourself to let go and come into the present moment. On the inhale, breathe in to honor the sacredness of your body and to come right into this healing temple under a lunar eclipse. It is perfectly safe, and you are protected by the highest light.

Imagine you can hear the background sound of the waves and feel the salt air purify your whole being—in particular, your second chakra. Bring your awareness to your left hand and ask for the power of the Blood Moon to charge the moonstone crystal you are holding so it is fully activated. Dissolve and transmute all wounding in your second chakra to clear all the hurt, injury, and pain that has accumulated during this lifetime or any other. See the energy, the red glow of the Blood Moon, pour down right into your second chakra. See the red glowing light melt away all wounding like a laser beam of love, transforming it into gratitude for your powerful creative center. State the following out loud or in your mind:

> My sacral chakra is completely healed, balanced, and restored to perfect functioning and health. I give myself full permission to experience joy, play, pleasure, and fun. All of my appetites are fully satisfied. My creativity, sexuality, and power are in optimal and harmonious balance on every level and in all directions of time.

Take a few breaths in and out to connect with this new state of healing, to fully upgrade to this new place of balance. Feel your second chakra rejuvenate beneath your left hand. Allow the moonstone crystal, supercharged by the lunar eclipse, to completely transform this beautiful center. Feel your vitality, your chi, being fully restored. Trust in every fiber of your being that it is so.

With your eyes still closed, bring your awareness to your renewed state of fortitude and health; begin to come back into your body by gently moving your legs, your arms, your feet, your hands. Take a few deep breaths and gently come back into the room. Let yourself integrate this powerful process by taking a few minutes to sit in stillness. Give thanks to your courageous self for going through this healing and to Mother Earth, Mother Ocean, and the great and powerful Blood Moon for all the support received. All is well, and you are whole.

Moon Worship

With your sacral chakra healed and your connection to your moon lineage restored, you are ready to live your life as the unapologetic heroine you are. Draw from this tale of Inanna and allow it to stir and awaken the goddess within. Let her work through you and witness the transformation that unfolds when you surrender to the power that is Inanna. Allow her to help you access your ability to confidently love your entire being.

Through the power of the Blood Moon, and with the help of the first daughter of the moon, you are now vibrating at the frequency of self-love. This frequency will be needed at the next gate, where we see Inanna gracefully erecting sacred boundaries to prevent the negative impact of external energy from others. She will demonstrate how, through sacred boundaries, to honor the self.

Gate Five

ERECTING SACRED BOUNDARIES

THE MYTH

Three Hymns to Inanna

These short hymns depict Inanna in three clear, distinct aspects of the Goddess, all as Venus moving through the sky. Venus is one of her many identities. Unlike the other myths, which are rooted in discrete narratives, these are fragmentary but no less comprehensive in their significance and application.

The cycle of Venus moving through its phases offers a useful metaphor for the ways in which boundaries can be used constructively. As Venus, Inanna's boundaries allow the integrated but separate aspects of her complexity and subjectivity to be showcased and to create the singularity of the role required for and during each phase. Contrary to most understandings of boundaries, we do not need to regard them as exclusionary. When erected with love, boundaries can actually enable synthesis and multiplicity—specifically because of the respect they encourage for the component parts of that whole.

In this way, boundaries are a safety mechanism that supports and protects through containment. In addition, they allow for clearly defined roles to be actualized in any given moment, leading to a solid sense of self. Let us turn to the hymns to explore how Inanna demonstrates strong sacred boundaries.

Hymn One: *The Lady of the Evening:* Inanna as Radiant Star

When the day ends, Inanna is seen as the transitional Great Light in the evening sky, clearly emphasizing her role in creating the conditions for repose and restoration. Her people engage in their ritual preparation for rest: "The men purify themselves; the women cleanse themselves."[63] Inanna invites all the beings of the land, the sea, and the sky to join her people in the move toward slumber. As they do, they give her offerings and raise their eyes to her. Joy is felt throughout the land. Connected to this joy is the art of sexual union that the Goddess inspires wherein "The young man makes love with his beloved,"[64] underscoring that a connection with the beloved is also a way to connect with and worship the Goddess. This refers to all sexual union and is not limited to heterosexual connection. Inanna's liminality extends through all aspects of being, including sexuality. The hymn ends with a prayer that is repeated across all three hymns: "I sing your praises, holy Inanna. /The Lady of the Evening is radiant on the horizon."[65]

Hymn Two: *The Lady Who Ascends into the Heavens:* Inanna as Lone Star

This hymn is a celebration and explanation of the ways in which Inanna is honored for her capacity to forge into uncharted territory while unapologetically taking time for herself by figuratively going within. It is through tending to herself that she can optimally tend to others. Inanna's people worship her ability to courageously ascend alone into the unknown of the heavens beyond their view. The hymn itemizes the many offerings left by her people in honor of her bravery and continued protection:

> They fill the table of the land with the first fruits.
> They pour dark beer for her.
> They pour light beer for her.[66]

She is brought holy sustenance, as "The gods and the people of Sumer go to her with food and drink."[67] Inanna's worshipers use ritual offerings to purify the land for her return in the hours before she reappears, and to fuel her. Reciprocal nourishment is at the heart of this hymn. Inanna's people nourish her in return for all she does to nourish them. We see this in the lines: "Flour, flour in honey, beer at dawn. / They pour wine and honey for her at sunrise."[68] Like the others, the hymn ends with a refrain of reverence for Inanna.

Hymn Three: *The Lady of the Morning:* Inanna as Honored Counselor

In this hymn, Inanna is celebrated for her role as initiator and guide, appearing in the sky "like bright daylight" as her people wake from slumber. In the morning, she is revered for her capacity to decree the fate of those seeking her counsel. She awakens them to the truth of their highest good:

When all the lands and the people of Sumer assemble,

Those sleeping on the roofs and those sleeping by the walls,

When they sing your praises, bringing their concerns to you,

You study their words.[69]

She assesses and punishes the ones who act in cruelty. However, the hymn describes her, "look[ing] with kindly eyes on the straightforward," and declares, "You give that one your blessing."[70] Her purpose during this aspect of her cycle is to act as a beacon, guiding those who seek her wisdom.

THE MYTH EXPLAINED

A Note About Boundaries

In the three hymns above, Inanna as Venus is depicted with her boundaries intact as she moves through the phases of Venus's planetary cycle. To fully comprehend these three hymns, we must understand the nature of sacred boundaries and what it means to have them in place.

It can be illustrative to understand boundaries in a professional context first. For example, in all types of therapeutic interventions, including psychotherapy, boundaries are crucial and part of an effective treatment plan that ensures the protection of both involved in the therapeutic dyad, creating a safe container for the therapeutic relationship and the intimacy and authenticity of emotional experience. This safe container mirrors the maternal holding environment, in which the client feels secure enough to surrender into the healing process. As therapists, we are charged with cultivating and guarding this sacred space. Thus, we must always do our own work to ensure that our own personal boundaries are solid and intact.

There are external boundaries and internal ones. External boundaries are in the material world and include the physical sense of where one person begins and another ends. In psychotherapy this includes, for example, the boundary of not having any other relationship with the client that is outside of the therapeutic connection, as well as the foundational precept of doing no harm. Internal boundaries are protective structures between you and yourself—the unseen demarcation between ego and what is not ego.

Constructive boundaries are in service of all involved. In the therapeutic setting, for example, it is essential to create a safe space for the client but also for the therapist. It is crucial that the therapist keep her own boundaries in check to be certain nothing surfaces to erode that safe space. If a therapist has porous boundaries, for instance, she may experience "compassion fatigue" in her work, or even resentment at how much her clients "need" her. In addition, without her own boundaries firmly established, she may misread what unfolds and create harm unintentionally.

Imagine the hypothetical situation of a client disclosing to the therapist that they have a crush on her. If her boundaries are intact, she knows that this crush is a form of projection, and she can help the client see this without feeling unnecessary shame or discomfort. In addition, she will not be at risk of becoming ungrounded by such a disclosure.

The therapist is many things all at once. She may also be a mother, a lover, and a friend in the world outside of the therapeutic setting. She does not disavow those other aspects of self when she is with her client. However, with her boundaries firmly in place, she can meet her client strictly from the identity most aligned with the client's healing—the therapist aspect of her identity. Constructive boundaries do not keep us from ourselves, they simply help us be who we are and allow us to share the aspect of ourselves that is aligned with where we are in any given moment. Again, it does not mean that we are not all those other aspects of self as well. We are indeed multidimensional.

Another lens through which to understand the importance of constructive boundaries is in the relationship between parent and child. There are times a child needs the boundaries of a parent to feel safe. As parents, we may think that the child always wants us to be accommodating and friend-like, conceding to whatever the child wants—until we see them slip into a tantrum of resistant, non-compliant behavior. But not having firm boundaries can actually make the child feel out of control and like they are spilling everywhere, unable to regulate their emotions. When we insist on boundaries and set limits as parents, the child experiences a sense of safety and containment.

A Solid Sense of Self

The three hymns underscore Inanna's multidimensionality, and, by association, our own. The paradox of integrating the many distinct aspects of ourselves is crucial for a balanced identity and what, in psychotherapy, we might conceptualize as a solid sense of self. Well-established boundaries allow us to develop this strong self-perception, wherein we are grounded and able to engage in a healthy relationship with self and others.

As she moves through her celestial cycle, Inanna is the perfect guide to teach us about boundaries. She demonstrates how having strong boundaries in place allows us to be fully present in the moment. Where our consciousness goes, our reality follows. As such, fully inhabiting the various aspects of our cycles through the assistance of well-established boundaries enhances our ability to be present, conscious, and positively impactful, and to make choices with clear intention that is aligned with the highest good for all. Inanna's worshippers demonstrate a deep respect for what she offers at any given moment, and they know that certain times of her cyclical nature correspond with specific gifts.

The Holy Trinity

In each of these three hymns, Inanna represents a different aspect of Venus in the sky. She is depicted in the evening after sunset, in the morning before sunrise, and as she disappears from our vision and ascends even higher into the heavens.

In Gates One through Four, we saw Inanna inhabiting the trinity of Maiden, Mother, and Crone. This tripartite structure even mimics the Goddess's three-syllabic name, its three *n*'s punctuating a distribution of self across an integrated whole. It is also reminiscent of the *vesica piscis* we have already explored, the two overlapping circles of the Divine Masculine and Divine Feminine that come together to create the almond-shaped, holy vulva intersection of the Divine Child.

The trinitarian aspects of Inanna, as well as this trilogy of hymns, symbolize the many as one. In doing so, they offer insights into employing boundaries to live authentically and multidimensionally.

And Venus was Her Name

Each of the discrete phases of Venus are clearly linked to a corresponding role Inanna plays in service of her people. The proximity of Venus to the Earth, as well as its thick, reflective clouds, make it the brightest planet and the third brightest luminous body in the sky. When we see Venus on the horizon, it is off to one side of the Sun in its orbital path. When we don't see Venus in the sky, it has gone behind or in front of the Sun.

Because Venus is close to our Sun, we can often see it in daylight—although it can be hard for the eye to locate. Venus follows a cycle of 584 days (called a synodic period) when it is seen as the morning star for 263 days, disappears for fifty days, and shows up again for 263 days as an evening star. Then it disappears again for eight days, and then the cycle is repeated.

There is a synergy, balance, and rhythm to this cycle. Inanna as Venus follows her own unique movements and invites us to emulate her, honoring ourselves by being fully present where we are in a specific aspect of our identity—such as mother, daughter, therapist, apprentice, or friend—and acknowledging the gifts that are associated with these aspects in the continuum of our being.

Inanna as Venus also teaches us about reflection. As Venus, she is a radiant light in the sky, yet this illumination is not generated from the planet itself but from the reflection of sunlight hitting the clouds surrounding it. Reflection is a central aspect of consciousness. One can argue that it is the doorway through which we enter consciousness. If reflection is defined as "using intention to think about something," the very alignment of intention and attention becomes consciousness.

Without reflection, we tend to behave on autopilot and are not operating with a great deal of consciousness. Metaphorically, as Venus reflects roughly seventy percent of the light hitting its surface, we too can transform the energy we receive and beam that light back out into the world, consciously engaging in weaving the dream of unity, peace, and love throughout our waking and sleeping states.

In the hymn *The Lady of the Evening*, we are told: "The people in all the lands lift their eyes to her."[71] Here, the radiant reflection of Venus commands attention. Her light transmits a blessing to her worshippers before they drift off to sleep. Because Inanna is the Goddess of Love, a blessing from her connects us with the heart. This connection reminds us to be fully conscious when we are dreaming. What are the dreams we want to have?

In *The Lady of the Morning*, Inanna beckons her people to the altars of the liminal:

> When all the lands and the people of Sumer assemble,
> Those sleeping on the roofs and those sleeping by the walls,
> When they sing your praises, bringing their concerns to you,
> You study their words.[72]

The rooftops and walls are at once symbols of the threshold (the same liminality that characterizes Inanna) and boundaries marking separateness. Sacred boundaries help us live in alignment. As Robert Frost writes in his poem "Mending Wall," "Good fences make good neighbors." [73] In the poem, Frost explores what he is "walling in or walling out" [74]— an echo of Inanna's wisdom. Like Frost, Inanna invites us to pause and consider the ways in which our sacred boundaries honor both self and other. With these boundaries, we protect our energy and ensure with intention that we take in only what aligns with our highest frequency.

The hymn *The Lady of the Morning* addresses Inanna directly in the line mentioned above: "You look with kindly eyes on the straightforward;/ You give that one your blessing."[75] Here, we see Inanna's favoring of straightforwardness as an expression of being fully present in the now. She honors those whose strong, sacred boundaries allow them to be right where they are.

Bring Her More Beer!

These hymns emphasize the offerings made to Inanna. Her worshippers' practice of nourishing her through their offerings is a symbolic gesture of nourishing themselves. In giving, we receive—just like Inanna gives the *me* to her people in the myth of *Inanna and the God of Wisdom,* explored in Gate Two. In return, Inanna is granted the role of supreme leader.

The practice of making offerings helps to regularly anchor us into the higher realms and to cultivate our connection to the Divine. When we intentionally make offerings to the Divine, whether at an altar or just in our thoughts, we sync our heart with our actions. This lifts our vibration. As such, every offering is also a gift to self.

INTERSECTION: UNDERSTANDING OUR OWN CHALLENGES THROUGH THE GODDESS OF LOVE

Boundaries

Many of us who are sensitive and empathic struggle with boundaries. We might walk a path of compassionate service through careers in the helping professions such as nursing, psychotherapy, or energy healing. We might also demonstrate our service as a mother, friend, lover, and conscious human. Our actions consistently reveal just how necessary it is to have those boundaries in place. Being empathic sets us up for wanting to support others at the expense of ourselves.

How often have you said "yes" when everything in you says "no"? How often have you given from a dry well? How often have you prioritized someone else over yourself? Struggling with boundaries can show up in all areas of your life—not just at work, where you may agree to stay later or take on more work than required because there is a need and you have the ability. It can show up in all relationships: romantic, parental, with your family of origin, among your friends, and even with your relationship to finances and your own body.

At the root of many porous boundaries are outdated patterns that we hold on to because they are familiar, albeit destructive. For example, this might mean a pattern of feeling conditionally worthy or deserving only if you give, support, do for, and say "yes." This might stem from, for example, an old childhood fear of getting in trouble. If you are a "people pleaser," the fear may be that if you assert yourself, you will be considered cold or "bitchy."

Or perhaps you consider yourself a peacekeeper and avoid confrontation to secure that identity. Porous boundaries beget even more porous boundaries, rather like a dam that gets broken—the water that seeps through destroys the dam even further.

If you struggle with boundaries, it can be a challenge just to go out into the world, especially in the current paradigm which is filled with the chaotic energy of change. Many intuitive and empathic individuals are deeply impacted energetically in crowded settings like a mall, concert, gym, or grocery store.

Having firm boundaries supports us in all ways, and ensures that we will not be overwhelmed and bombarded by all the energy swirling around in the ethos because such energy is not aligned with us. We must also be mindful to protect ourselves from projections that may be directed at us, but are not actually about us at all.

Understanding Projection

Weak boundaries can lead to taking things personally. In psychotherapy, we understand that on some level, everything is a projection. We are a synthesis of our experiences, and these experiences impact how we perceive and understand our world. The concept of projection was brought to light by Sigmund Freud.[76]

Projection is a defense mechanism to express emotions that we repress. In addition, it pertains to that which we resist or dislike within ourselves, even if it is not actually repressed. In this case, we may project the undesired quality or attribute onto someone else, externalizing it so we can observe it safely outside of ourselves. There are also very innocuous projections we engage all the time; for example, a tech-savvy individual might assume that technology makes perfect sense to all of us.

Projection and Relationships

As you begin to understand projection, you will notice greater ease in erecting sacred boundaries. As energetic tools, sacred boundaries envelop you within a protective field, enhancing your capacity to honor and respect yourself. They protect you from the impact of disempowering energy aimed in your direction by way of projection, making it easier to gain perspective and develop compassion.

Boundaries allow you to see how projection originates from a place of wounding and unresolved emotions in other beings, ensuring that you do not take things personally. Sacred boundaries, therefore, enable us to dissolve tension by staying grounded. They allow us to demonstrate, by positive example, what it looks like to have boundaries firmly in place.

Having insufficient boundaries within relationships can lead to feelings of being taken advantage of—as though one person is always giving and the other is receiving. This dynamic can show up in our romantic relationships and our friendships, leading us to feel taxed by these connections instead of uplifted and supported. As parents, not having sacred boundaries can result in feeling enmeshed with the child, leading to a lack of independence on the part of the child or a reversal of roles. All of this can have an impact on the child's sense of self and future relationships. In our relationships with our family of origin, porous boundaries may cause us to take on the energy of our loved ones, potentially perpetuating wounding through our generational lineage.

Boundaries impact all our relationships, not just the ones we have with individuals. They can also impact our relationships with our bodies or even with money. Imagine, for instance, that you give your services away for free or at an overly reduced rate because you "feel" the financial struggle of the other. With respect to your body, this may take the form of pushing it beyond what it is capable of. You might sacrifice your rest, nutrition, and hydration. You might overextend yourself to support others, while not feeling able to speak up for and honor your own needs.

A lack of boundaries can lead us to engaging in unhealthy lifestyle behaviors such as excess caffeine or eating poorly, because there is no time to prepare something nourishing, no time to work out, no time to sleep, no time to play and have fun—in other words, no time to prioritize the self. What are the patterns that are keeping you from having solid boundaries? With whom do boundaries feel the most challenging to keep in place?

More Energy, Less Drama

Sacred boundaries are a self-care tool. When you prioritize good boundaries, you will have access to increased energy and will feel more centered. Doing so can help you live in the present instead of the past. When you prioritize strong, sacred boundaries, you will stop taking things personally. You'll disengage from triggered reactivity. This will contribute to cultivating more peace in your own life and, in turn, help restore peace on the planet. With sacred boundaries firmly in place, we can ensure that we allow in only those vibrations that align with our highest good and support our ability to develop equanimity.

Upgrade Your Armor to That of a Goddess

In the process of inhabiting your role as an unapologetic heroine helping to restore the Divine Feminine consciousness our planet needs, you must ensure you are appropriately protected. With the armor of sacred boundaries, we are more capable of staying the course in the face of challenging situations. This doesn't mean we can't feel stress or sadness, or that challenges cease to exist. But we can interface with those scenarios differently. We can take things less personally and not be so easily triggered.

By using conscious intention to keep our sacred boundaries strong, we cultivate an upgraded relationship with ourselves.

Why Boundaries Might be Hard for Us

Trauma can impact our ability to establish solid boundaries. Trauma directly affects our sense of safety and can include physical or emotional harm or even the threat of harm, experienced either briefly or in an ongoing manner.

Many circumstances can feel traumatic, including all types of abuse, bullying, death, natural disasters, and even past-life experiences that are carried into this life. In other words, your boundaries might have been significantly violated in this life or in many past lives, leaving an energetic imprint in your current field. This may be at the root of your difficulties in establishing and maintaining boundaries in the present. However, it is definitely possible to restore them.

THE HEALING INTERVENTION

Erecting sacred boundaries is correlated with the first chakra or root chakra. This energy center is connected to our identity and to feeling safe in the world. As you heal and balance this center, your sense of safety increases, fostering your ability to share your true identity with the world, free of defense mechanisms.

Ritual for Erecting Sacred Boundaries

Items required: A few pieces of paper, a pen, sage/smudge stick, any kind of bowl, and a space outside where there are trees. If you live in a city, try to find a quiet corner of a local park. Invite the trees to be a part of your circle to help bear witness to your process and to help you erect sacred boundaries around yourself. They will help you feel safe by surrounding you protectively and mirroring how to stand firmly and with authority, as they are thoroughly grounded in their network of root systems. Ask them for their support with this ritual and open your heart to their magnificent power. Trust they have heard your request and are willing to help you. Send them love from your heart in gratitude. State the following prayer three times:

> May Inanna teach me the way to erect and keep firm sacred boundaries in all aspects of my life.

STEP 1. Before you take a seat in whatever natural space you chose, just stand for a moment. Call in your guides to be present and join forces with the sacred trees around you. With your eyes closed, imagine you hear your own guides communicating to you along with the trees. Imagine them assembling before you. Still standing and with eyes closed, feel one of your guides place their hand on the top of your head. Their hand is emitting the most radiant light. This light feels like liquid gold pouring in through your crown chakra and flowing all the way down, through every aspect of your being, right down through your feet, and extending out through the soles of your feet into the Earth. Notice this strong sense of rootedness and protection. Now take a seat.

STEP 2. Open your eyes, knowing your guides are present and ready to assist you. Ask for their assistance in releasing and transmuting outdated patterns that may be causing porous boundaries that are no longer in alignment with your heart or your highest good and healing.

STEP 3. Sit in meditation with a notebook. Ask your guides if there are any outdated patterns in this life or in any past incarnations that are still active and showing up in the present moment as a block to sacred boundaries. Close your eyes and sit in silence as your guides inform you.

You might hear, see, know, or feel what they are showing you. Receive. Write down what comes to you. Ask your guides to help enlighten you. What patterns or behaviors that may have impacted your ability to erect sacred boundaries are no longer serving you? Check in with your free will and decide if you are ready to let them go. Ask yourself if you are ready to fully release and transmute these outdated patterns. Sit and let yourself process for as long as you need.

STEP 4. After identifying what patterns might be causing porous boundaries, write out each on one on a piece of paper. Feel free to use as many sheets of paper as needed. For example, these may be patterns such as:

It is my responsibility to take care of everyone around me.

I don't deserve to prioritize myself; everyone else comes before me.

If I don't prove my hard work ethic, I will not be valued.

I am a peacekeeper and am only valuable if I am helping someone.

If I disappoint someone, they will no longer love me.

Turn to face the trees now and move closer to them. Hold the paper in front of you while placing your left hand on your heart. Then state the following aloud:

I officially and with pure intention fully release and let go of these patterns now and in all directions of time. All are instantly transmuted into love and directed into the soil to help nourish all the trees on our planet. I honor myself and my integrity to do what is in line with my heart. I honor myself through strong and firm, sacred boundaries.

Tear the paper up into small pieces and throw these pieces into the bowl. After the ritual is done, sage them before recycling them. You can do so by lighting a sage bundle and encircling the bowl with the smoke to purify the energy therein.

STEP 5. Know in your heart that it is done. State aloud three times:

All is balanced and complete. All is balanced and complete. All is balanced and complete. I am perfectly grounded with firm and solid, sacred boundaries in place that serve to honor me in every way.

STEP 6. In gratitude to yourself and to your guides who showed up to support you, extend your arms out at your sides, palms facing outward. Intentionally send love from your heart out through your hands in a gesture of open and generous appreciation. Bow to the trees before you and send a prayer to them for their protection and well-being.

With all our old patterns released and with firm boundaries erected, we are now able to offer an intention to live unapologetically. If the following resonates with your heart and feels like an authentic way in which to conduct your life, allow it to be a guiding mantra, an intention to orient you as you walk the path of living unapologetically:

> I live from the highest level of consciousness I have access to in this now moment. I love myself and live unapologetically so that I may be a pure instrument through which unconditional love and light is shared with the world, while I embody sacred boundaries solidly established within myself. These sacred boundaries support and protect me on my path. The Earth is restored through my own inner balance. I live the truth that we are all one and, as such, I hold my heart open to the freedom, peace, healing, protection, joy, and fulfillment of all sentient beings of this world and all other worlds. I honor myself and respect the sacred boundaries of all. My intention, prayer, thought, speech, and action are perfectly aligned with the highest good and healing of all beings now and in all directions of time.

Let Your Roots Spread Love

Connecting with the trees in the ritual above helped you align with your own root energy of your first chakra, to strengthen and balance it. This is a central aspect to establishing strong boundaries. The ritual enabled you to manifest these boundaries. You are ready now to go forward feeling safe in the world, knowing that you are protected by honoring your boundaries. This helps you to be grounded through your first chakra, allowing you to be more fully in your body.

In Gate Six, Inanna demonstrates her refusal to be bound. She transcends the binary to own and honor her multidimensionality. Now that you feel safer in the world, you can join Inanna and explore how you might do the same!

Gate Six

TRANSCENDING THE BINARY

THE MYTH

The Holy One

In Gate Five, we explored three short but impactful hymns. Here, too, we will examine a similarly short yet far-reaching hymn. *The Holy One* begins in festivity. The people of Sumer stage a celebratory parade to the rhythmic beat of the drum and resonating chords of the harp. Colorfully adorned and beautifully made up, the young men carry hoops and the women carry swords and axes. The people of Sumer begin their processional. An anchoring refrain of "I say, 'Hail!' to Inanna, First Daughter of the Moon!" is echoed and interchanged with the variant: "I say, 'Hail!' to Inanna, Great

Lady of Heaven!"[77] These two utterances assert Inanna's dominance in the pantheon of Sumerian gods and identify her as the guide for the cultural evolution and collective transformation of the people of Sumer.

Significantly, Inanna's worshippers dress to honor her acceptance of and reverence for the non-binary and gender fluidity. Inanna's holy office encompasses the inclusivity of all identifications, including those who might identify, in our current-day terminology, as non-binary, genderqueer, and transgender. Indeed, she consecrates those who identify as whomever they feel most aligned with, regardless of the gender they were ascribed at birth. Inanna's worshippers revere sensuality as a sacred medium to connect with the Divine:

> The male prostitutes comb their hair before you.
> They decorate the napes of their necks with colored scarfs,
> They drape the cloak of the gods about their shoulders.[78]

By defying strict categorizations of gender representation, Inanna's followers concretize the sacred act of balancing masculine and feminine energy. In so doing, they embody the authenticity and wisdom of the unified heart. We see this in the following lines:

> The women adorn their right side with men's clothing.
> The people of Sumer parade before you.
> I say "Hail!" to Inanna, Great Lady of Heaven!
> The men adorn their left side with women's clothing.[79]

Through the power of ceremony, Inanna inspires her people to prioritize integration and balance and unite in collectively challenging limiting social constructs.

Gate Six: Transceding the Binary

The joyous procession moves toward Inanna's temple, with participants singing and jumping rope as they go. Once they arrive at Inanna's majestic throne, they begin a symbolic ritual of sacrifice—a simultaneous act of death and rebirth. The sacrifice is aligned with the ceremonial music, as the notes of the drums and tambourines guide the worshippers through the figurative gesture of offering their own life(blood) to her as one priest uses his sword [exactly how is unclear] to mark the group's blood-tie commitment to Inanna.

Ultimately, they arrive at their destination: the goddess. The music resonates through their bodies, as if they have been activated by their newly integrated wholeness. The hymn continues:

> The ascending kurgarra priests raise their swords before you.
> The priest, who covers his sword with blood, sprinkles blood,
> He sprinkles blood over the throne of the court chamber.
> The tiki-drum, the sem-drum, and the ala-tambourine resound.[80]

The sacrificial offering of blood is marked by a thundering crescendo of the percussive instruments, all in reverence to the Goddess of Love. This can be interpreted not as a human or animal sacrifice, but rather an offering that is connected to the lineage of the goddess—an honoring of the potency of womb power through the symbolic blood of menses.

The hymn ends with a celebration of Inanna, who looks from her place in the heavens "...in sweet wonder on all the lands."[81] Her gaze is a gesture of inclusivity. Inanna is the inspiration to come together in a deliberate attempt to dissolve the normative boundaries of gender. In the beam of her light, she ensures *everyone* is seen as sacred.

THE MYTH EXPLAINED

The Holy One is not actually about a monolithic "one" at all. Rather, the hymn celebrates fluidity—specifically, gender fluidity. By defying strict categorizations of gender representation and roles, the hymn conceptually posits the expansive capacity of an alternative to the binary—a third category that liberates, integrates, and reflects the generative potentiality of the in-between.

A masterful reconciling of self is depicted in the hymn, which is an artistic rendering that emphasizes the sanctity of transcending the binary of gender identification. The hymn is marked by a distinct refusal to be bound and a continuous emphasis on blurring lines.

In her role as the Holy One, Inanna consecrates the non-binary, celebrating the courageous act of identifying and representing oneself in congruence with one's heart. Although pertaining to gender here, the wider message is one of transcending binaries of all kinds—even while honoring the energetic boundaries we explored in Gate Five. The "one-ness" of this hymn, then, can be seen as unity consciousness both outwardly and within—in any given moment, we can all be many.

Two Roads Diverged, and Inanna Travels the One Between

Percussive sound is used to enhance an altered state of consciousness throughout the myths and hymns of Inanna, both symbolically through the mention of drums or drumming, as well as in the syllabic rhythm and tonal frequency of the language. The percussive instruments in the ceremony act as an invitation to rhythmically align with the heartbeat of the cosmos and the heartbeat of the goddess.

Although we are reading the myths in translation from Sumer, it is hard not to imagine that the soothing vibrational aspects of the texts are intentional—no matter our native language. At the very least, where repetition occurs, such as in a refrain, the sonic undulation of the language can synchronize and balance us. The experience of reading the myths and hymns of the goddess, and particularly reading them aloud, can help tune the body, mind, and spirit.

Throughout the hymn, the people of Sumer acknowledge and embody the balance and authenticity that Inanna exemplifies and espouses. By being her authentic self, Inanna has brought their culture into a harmonious congruence. Such congruence refers to an alignment between a person's inner experience and self-image and their outer experience and self-expression.

As we saw in Gate Five, Inanna celebrates the many different aspects of self, as depicted in her tripartite rendering of Venus moving through her cycles in the sky. Her trinitarian aspects are present in this hymn as well.

In *The Holy One*, the trinity consists of the masculine, feminine, and non-binary, including all self-identity that comes from the heart, regardless of whether it is aligned with one's gender ascribed at birth. One's identity might not fit within traditional categories of male and female, and Inanna both identifies and honors this truth. Prioritizing the inclusion and acceptance of all forms and expressions of the non-binary encourages unity consciousness. Several scholars have highlighted the fact that Inanna not only possesses the power to transform gender, which we will explore below, but also that she represents the androgyny of the non-binary by embodying her polarities.[82]

Inner Marriage

Throughout the parade, the people of Sumer pay tribute to Inanna's own balancing of the masculine and feminine within. The women wear typically masculine clothing on the right side of their bodies, while the men don traditionally female clothing on their left side. Through this gesture, the people of Sumer symbolically enact congruence and balance. Additionally, the hoops carried by the men are evocative of the circular, womb-like shape of the feminine, while the axes and swords the women carry are phallic.

This depiction demonstrates another inversion of hegemonic codes of gender. In the hands of men, these hoops connect the masculine with the generative/creative energy of the feminine to honor this aspect within. The swords carried by the women symbolize an ability to penetrate the truth or to pass on one's seed of truth.

The inner marriage of our Divine Masculine and Divine Feminine yields the Divine Child—the healed and most powerful version of ourselves. Through this balancing, we embody our Divinity on the Earth plane, establishing a connection with the cosmos to merge with the All That Is. In so doing, we become connected to the master plan of unity and can positively support it.

Inanna's myths remind us that when we alter one aspect of the universe, the entire sacred geometry of it is altered. Inanna empowers us by demonstrating how effective we can be as agents of change.

Womb Wisdom is Inclusive

As the daughter of the Moon, Inanna is a womb priest/ess.[83] The moon is linked to the feminine cycle of menstruation, with its 29.5-day lunar cycle. Inanna's parents are both moon gods; thus, the lunar/menstrual cycle is part of her ancestral line. Additionally, as Goddess of Love and sexual love, Inanna's second chakra—her womb center—is vibrant, which means she has access to her sexuality and her desire for sacred union. As such, she stands before us as a gateway to unity.

When the priest in the hymn "covers" his sword in blood and "sprinkles blood over the throne," he is honoring the regenerative aspects of the feminine in relationship to the phallic image of sword, a symbolic merger of the feminine and masculine forces. By making a symbolic gesture of spreading this blood over Inanna's throne, the priest can be seen as highlighting Inanna's capacity for creation, her sacred womb lined with potent, transformative blood, which has given birth to a newly balanced culture.

As the Goddess of Love, Inanna prioritizes the heart as the main directional center of the body. The vibrational alignment between the heart and how we identify in all aspects of our being allows us to be who we truly are. Inanna's teaching, which is central to the path of mastery, insists that the heart be the deciding factor in every choice we make, rather than arbitrary and restricting cultural confines. Congruence within and without is one of Inanna's primary messages, marking her as one of the earliest teachers of ascension.

Ceremony as a Gateway to Inanna

The hymn ends with Inanna beaming her love light from the celestial sphere onto her worshippers. At the end of the hymn, we realize we have just witnessed a ceremony of the people of Sumer. Once her priests and priestesses convene, they walk together in a moving meditation.

Because Inanna's path is not a rigid one, their meditative state is also playful as they make their way to her throne. The destination is her temple, likely in her city of Uruk, where they go to make an offering of sacrificial blood. The sacrifice is a symbolic gesture of giving their life to her through blood, thereby becoming linked to her so she can assist in their individual process of rebirth. Again, this can be interpreted as an honoring of her creative, generative energy.

The end of the procession brings them to the perfect vantage point of the rising of Venus in the darkening sky. As they walk to meet her, the people progressively merge with the energy of Inanna, first through their dress, then through the meditative movement and play of their procession, and then through the percussive instruments that serve to usher them into an altered state in which to connect with the wisdom she offers.

Inanna's shining light can be understood as the luminous permission to her worshippers to act as she does, true to self. The light of Venus shining down raises the collective vibration.

INTERSECTION: UNDERSTANDING OUR OWN CHALLENGES THROUGH THE GODDESS OF LOVE

Inanna Transcends the Binary

One of the most prominent ways Inanna is a symbol for the unapologetic heroine is through her refusal to be bound. This can be interpreted in many ways, including sexual orientation and gender identity. Inanna/Venus is always shifting as she moves through the sky. She cannot be held down or defined because she is always creating herself anew. She embodies what author Lars Muhl calls the "Isogynic Being,"[84] the balanced synergy of the masculine and feminine aspects of self. This is a potent teaching and it is why, as a goddess of the liminal, Inanna is all things and nothing at once. She embodies the need for inclusivity and uses her platform to cultivate it, just as the poet Enheduanna did in her honor more than 4,000 years ago.

Ultimately, this inclusivity leads to unity, a reflection of congruence within and without. Fortunately, today there is a resurgence in the collective refusal to be bound. One of the ways this is evident is in the capacity to transcend binary gender identification. With her multiple epitaphs and multidimensionality, Inanna exemplifies the self-acceptance that begets unity. She returns today to command unity consciousness and decree the fate of humanity toward this end.

A Poetess Speaks

The long poem "Lady of Largest Heart" was written by Enheduanna, a priestess and the first recorded author, whom we met in the introduction "Freefall: Finding Your Bearings." In this poem, we see Inanna's capacity to help us rise above limitation. The poet, who lived and wrote between 2285 and 2250 BCE, reveals Inanna's capacity to ordain the wise and courageous ones who know who they are and live their truth:

> over the maiden's head
> she makes a sign of prayer
> hands then folded at her nose
> she declares her manly/woman.[85]

Inanna uses a powerful gesture of transformation—a mudra—that elicits an attunement above the head of the maiden turned "manly/woman." This is done at the crown chakra, connecting the person more deeply with their mighty "I Am" Presence—their individual active expression of Source-consciousness and perfection.[86]

Enheduanna continues:

> in sacred rite
> she takes the broach

which pins a woman's robe
breaks the needle, silver thin
consecrates the maiden's heart as male
gives to her a mace
for this one dear to her
she shifts a god's curse
a blight reversed
out of nothing shapes
what has never been
her sharp wit
splits the door
where cleverness resides
and there reveals
what lives inside.[87]

Here, Enheduanna describes a sacred ritual the goddess is known for, in which Inanna formally supports one of her worshippers in their transition from identifying as female to identifying as male. Inanna hears the hearts of her worshippers and supports them in their process of stepping into their most salient identity.

The next section of the poem continues, "For this one dear to her/ she shifts a god's curse." Inanna then blesses this individual for their courage and ensures this one receives her Divine intervention for a smooth transition. In the lines, "out of nothing shapes/ what has never been," Enheduanna highlights Inanna's ability to see in a new way and to offer up the transcendent choice that defies limitation.

Finally, in the lines "her sharp wit/ splits the door/ where cleverness resides," Enheduanna captures the essence of Inanna's power, which is the ability to cut through illusion and access the truth. When you work with Inanna's energy, you can zero in on the truth with the precision and skill of a goddess.

When we have come into balance within ourselves, our relationships begin to reflect this. Romantic relationships become opportunities for transmutation, echoing the connections of our foremothers and fathers, like Inanna and Dumuzi, Isis and Osiris, and Jesus and Mary.

I want to underscore that this is not necessarily about a heterosexual connection. This is possible in every single type of love connection, regardless of gender, gender identification, or sexual orientation. For a balanced individual, all relationships become an opportunity to evolve, but the relationship with the beloved becomes a reflection of the sacred union accessed within the self. In this way, love can lead to alchemical transformation for both individuals. We must always start with the self.

Into the Looking Glass

The path of living unapologetically is an invitation to live an integrous life. Relationships are a path to this congruence, because all relationships are a mirror. Gaze into that looking glass with eyes wide open. If you train yourself to look for opportunities to move toward greater inner harmony, you will see them show up everywhere.

Ask your higher self to show you opportunities to develop more congruence, and trust what comes forward. Be aware of the stubborn defense mechanisms which may try to tell you everything is already aligned. In other words, be willing to be completely honest with yourself. There is no judgment. Let go of all fear around what you might see in yourself and the lack of alignment you may witness.

It can be challenging to walk this path because of the ego, which often pulls us out of our heart and into fear. We may, for example, never act unkindly toward others but act viciously toward ourselves. We may eat clean foods but binge on alcohol. We may tell others of the importance of boundaries but let our own be breached regularly. There is no judgment in such revelations. We took a human incarnation with the intention to learn how to live in human form while simultaneously walking in spiritual alignment. This is part of our creative play.

For those who believe in reincarnation, coming into the world of form is, by definition, challenging. This is because when we become incarnate, we do not fully remember all the plans we mapped out in that higher dimensional reality between lives. This is due to the veil of amnesia. It can feel like driving somewhere without a map.

You must develop an inner guidance system to find the way. Be gentle with yourself, have patience, and drop all inner judgment about the ways in which you may be out of alignment. Simply try to proactively shift closer to congruence in an open-hearted way. Be your own most unconditionally loving mother. Such a mother would be patient and supportive of a child who is behaving in a way that is not oriented to truth, peace, or love. She would gently, and perhaps repeatedly, demonstrate a more evolved response until the child can finally follow the mother's guidance. Regardless, such guidance always comes from a stance of unconditional love.

Trust Your Intuition

Trusting in your own intuition is key. In your heart, you know who you are. If you are reading this book, you are incredibly intuitive. You heard the inner call to connect the messages herein to assist you in embodying the wisdom of the Goddess of Love on the planet.

You can connect directly with the higher realms and receive the guidance that exists for you. You just have to trust. Every time the self-doubt emerges, lean in and consciously choose to override it.

Remember that whenever you pause and go within to access the guidance you are seeking, you strengthen the feedback loop. The more you do it, the stronger your gift of intuition becomes. Your higher self wrote your destiny and knows exactly where you are headed and who you are. Give yourself the permission to be that person and share your truth with the world. The more you ask your higher self what next step you need to take, the more easily you will be able to hear that guiding wisdom.

It can be helpful to rely on the support of skilled practitioners in the emotional clearing and healing work you do; yet hearing your own truth is something *you* are best at doing on your own. Have faith in this fact. As you continue to engage in your own truth and to rely upon it, you will strengthen your own discernment. Let your discernment help you transcend any felt limitations that may exist for you. Live your truth.

The Tools of Sacred Practice

As is highlighted by the hymn *The Holy One*, ceremony and ritual are significant and impactful ways to concretize an internal shift. From simple to elaborate, and anything in between, using ceremony and ritual to cultivate transformation is something that can be done free of charge and on one's own.

Ceremony and ritual are done through accessing the energetic realm, a place in which evolution occurs with great speed. The people of Sumer regularly engaged with the Divine realm, and they did so with intention. Indeed, in ancient Sumer, each city showcased the temple of its ruling god or goddess, which was its focal point. It housed the statue of the god or goddess and included an altar for worship and offerings.[88]

In the hymn, we see various tools used in ceremony, from the specific adornment of Inanna's worshippers to the swords of the priests, the hoops carried by the young men, the double-edged axes carried by the young women, and the specific musical instruments chosen and played—the harp and drums. Tools used in ceremony and ritual can literally and figuratively activate a connection with the Divine. In the hymn, these tools help the worshippers align with Inanna/Venus, acting like a bridge to her energy and her essence of inclusivity and unity.

As you contemplate ways to make manifest your most authentic truth, consider what tools might be of assistance. Perhaps crystals are your preferred channel. Or you might prefer the Tarot, a pendulum, a rattle, a drum, a cauldron, a medicine basket, a statue, or an altar. Now is the time to listen to and get a feel for what resonates as a means of assisting you at this beautiful and exciting point of your journey.

All of the tools mentioned are meant to be used with the utmost respect and highest regard. They hold great power, so use them with care. Commit to their use only for the highest good and healing of all. Treat the process of selecting your tools as though you are meeting a new spiritual teacher. Honor them as such with a commitment to using them for your evolution. Sage your tools by encircling them with the smoke of a lit smudge stick to "clear" them and allow them to sync with your own energy. Leave them in the moonlight or sunlight for an hour or more until you *feel* as if they have been fully cleared and positively charged. You can also bless them, or use Reiki or prayer over them.

HEALING INTERVENTION

Transcending the binary is a sixth chakra, third eye issue. It involves accessing the inner sight necessary to see beyond the confines of limiting, socially-constructed norms. Your discernment allows you to pierce through fear, illusion, and anything that stands in the way of your sovereignty, so that you may clearly see the truth of your own heart.

As we have learned in this powerful hymn, Inanna possess the ability to ordain an individual's process of owning their salient identity. The following ritual is meant to help facilitate your own process of consecrating your truest and most congruent expression of self, placing the power to do so in your own hands. You can perform this ritual once, monthly, or yearly, depending on where you are in your individual process of self-acceptance. You might find it serves you well to do this ritual monthly for six months and then move to doing it yearly to simply reinforce your intention to live with a heart-centered focus, unrestrained by external limitations.

Ritual for Congruence: You are The Holy One

This ritual should be done at dusk on a clear evening when you can see the planet Venus in the darkening sky. If Venus is currently shining as the Morning Star instead of the Evening Star in the place where you live, you can also do it before sunrise as Venus lights up the morning sky. Congratulate yourself for your willingness to let go of what may have blocked congruence in your past and open yourself to the freedom of living your truth unapologetically.

This ritual will look different for everyone. You can perform this ritual alone or together with your soul team in your honor. Your soul team is your circle of friends or family who support you.

Taking a cue from the hymn, use the symbolic gesture of fashion to represent your inner balance. Inanna's worshippers emphasize both balance and androgyny—dissolving the binary by blurring lines of separation through their attire, the fashion they use for self-expression.

This is a ritual of celebration. If you have tambourines, drums, or other percussive instruments, use these. If your celebration includes the presence of others, perhaps it can be done around a fire pit. If you are doing this ritual celebration alone, wear something that feels festive and priest/ess-like—whatever that means to you. If you don't have a fire pit, simply place a candle on the ground. As we go through the steps below you will be using flowers to create a circle around the fire.

Items required: A drink—either beer, which was often used in Sumer as an offering to Inanna, or wine, juice, or water in a special glass; nine flowers, or a single flower with at least nine petals; your sacred journal; and an outdoor space. As you read this, you may become aware of a tool that seems to call out to you. If you intuitively feel resonance with a particular sacred tool to use in this ritual, by all means include that as well. State the following prayer aloud three times:

> May Inanna consecrate my unlimited nature and help me
> see that I am holy and perfect in every way.

STEP 1. Ask Inanna, Queen of Heaven and Earth, and all higher-dimensional beings who are connected to you and who are committed to the protection, healing, and guidance of the Earth plane, to join you.

STEP 2. Imagine grounding cords emerging from your feet to safely secure you into the energy of the Earth, establishing your centered connection to your own core and the core of the planet.

STEP 3. Either standing or sitting, close your eyes. Imagine yourself as a priest/ess of Inanna, a Holy One yourself, a being who has transcended the binary and lives beyond limitation. In your mind's eye, see yourself holding the Holy Grail, represented by a chalice held at your heart center. Overflowing from the chalice is radiant, golden light. The vibrancy of this light merges with your heart, and its energy engulfs your whole being. This light causes you to you remember who you are; to remember your truth; and to have the courage to live that truth fully. The Holy Grail is the feminine consciousness that serves all of humanity and helps you give yourself permission to live your truth beyond all limitation. The chalice signifies the womb, marking the generative energy available to birth your true, unique expression, your most congruent and balanced you.

In your mind's eye, imagine the light in this chalice is liquid light. Hold it up in a gesture of offering to Inanna and take a sip, drawing this light into you, thereby merging with the generative energy within and without, to restore balance and bring you into congruence. Allow the golden light within the Holy Grail to illuminate your truth and fill you with the ability to embody it always.

STEP 4. Light the candle or the fire. Take the nine flowers or nine petals, and place them evenly in a circle around the outside of the fire pit or candle. This circle of flowers figuratively represents the nine gestational months within the womb. You are becoming your most congruent, unlimited self.

STEP 5. Read the following prayer aloud three times:

> I honor myself fully and give myself permission to share my authentic truth with the world. I love who I am and accept myself exactly as I am. I now instantly let go of anything that has historically blocked my ability to live true to myself. All old and outdated blocks dissolve instantly and are transmuted into peace. I have the courage to be me and express myself in alignment with my heart on every level and in all ways. I now willingly and joyfully receive all gifts, codes, keys, activations, wisdom, and blessings from Inanna that are aligned with my current level of readiness. I am fully congruent on every level and in all directions of time. I walk my path of truth with honor, committing to inspire others to do the same. I see the beauty and interconnection of all things. Balance and peace are restored in me and Mother Earth. I celebrate my courage and strength to live my truth.

STEP 6. Now toast in celebration of your ability to embody the wisdom of Inanna and, most important, your own heart. Drink your drink and toast to yourself or the soul team you have assembled. Pour some of your drink around the outside of the circle, sharing it with Inanna in appreciation of her support. Acknowledge that you join her in helping to uplift humanity and honor yourself for this commitment.

STEP 7. Give thanks to Inanna, all the Divine beings who came to support you, your soul team, yourself, and Mother Earth for helping ground this transformation in you.

Anchor in Your Congruence

Upon completion of your ritual, take a few moments to feel your own inspiration. How did participating in this ritual impact you? Did you notice any resistance or inner judgment show up—and if so, how did you push beyond it? Did you experience your own power to sanctify yourself? Were you able to surrender fully into the ritual? Consider your process and what showed up for you in the ritual.

Use your sacred journal to write down feelings that may have surfaced. This will be your personal recording of your felt experience of this powerful process. Having these notes will help you with the next step, which is anchoring in your congruence through your own artistic expression.

Much of what we know about Inanna comes from art, the written word, myths, hymns, and poetry, as well as carvings and cylinder seals of her likeness that were made in her honor and preserved through the years. These artifacts have resurfaced at precisely the right time, as we now need her help more than ever in moving toward unity consciousness. Through these media she speaks to us, and the art itself acts as a portal to connect with her directly.

In this vein, create an artistic work that captures you as a limitless, authentic, and integrous guide and inspiration for humanity. In doing so, you are creating a work of art that will serve as a portal back to the energy of this ritual. Your creation will help you to connect with the congruent state that the ritual facilitated; it can be used to solidify this state throughout all aspects of your emotional, mental, spiritual, and physical bodies. Your work of art can be used at any time when you feel self-doubt emerge and want to anchor back into that state of confident congruence.

You can create the artwork immediately after the ritual, but it might better support you to deepen the experience over the next several days.

Commit to carving out the time to write a poem, or maybe a letter to yourself reflecting your awe at your own courage. Perhaps you wish to create a song, or draw, paint, or use photography to capture your limitless, expansive truth and nature.

You may simply choose to take a picture of your ritual, capturing the flowers spread in a circle, the celebratory clothing you have donned, and you standing in congruence. Once completed, place this artwork next to your bed so it can help you weave the inspiration of your congruence into your dream and waking worlds simultaneously, helping to anchor you in on every level. Just as the people of Sumer used artistic renderings of their gods and goddesses as a way to connect with the Divine, your artwork can help you stay in tune with your authentic and congruent self-expression.

We are all works of art—and through art we can inspire ourselves to live as the Divine creators we are.

Stand With the Goddess

With your ritual completed to honor your congruence and support your ability to chart the path that is uniquely your own, you are equipped with the inner strength to be who you are at a soul level. You now stand alongside Inanna as an embodiment of transcending limitation. It is your time to live unbound as your authentic self.

This process helped to strengthen your sixth chakra, your powerful third eye. When this center is balanced, it allows for the discernment needed to see yourself clearly so you can feel empowered and withstand any unconscious pull toward the old paradigm. You are ready to move to the next gate, wherein Inanna goes through her ascension process and teaches us how to rise.

Gate Seven

SURRENDER TO ASCEND

THE MYTH

The Descent of Inanna continued, The Dream of Dumuzi, and The Return.

Thinking back to Gate One, you will recall that we left off in *The Descent of Inanna* just as Inanna rises from the dead. At that point, the story then gets even more interesting. We will now pick up that story here. Resurrected, Inanna begins to make her way out of the underworld and confronts the Annuna. These are the judges of the Great Below. They explain to her that in order to leave the underworld, someone must take her place. She pushes onward, while *galla*—which are demons of the underworld— cling to her side, ready to claim her replacement.

Stepping into the world above, Inanna sees her dear counselor Ninshubur dressed in mourning. Ninshubur immediately falls at her feet. The *galla* reach for Ninshubur, ready to take her as Inanna's replacement. But Inanna protests, citing Ninshubur's faithful devotion and role in her resurrection.

Still accompanied by the *galla*, Inanna, and Ninshubur continue to the city of Umma, where they encounter Inanna's son, Shara. He is also dressed in mourning and lamenting her loss, and he also falls at Inanna's feet in reverence. Again, the *galla* proclaim that Shara is a worthy replacement for Inanna, but she refuses: "He is my son, who sings hymns to me."[89]

As they continue to the city of Badtibira, they encounter Inanna's son, Lulal. He, too, is dressed in mourning and grieving her loss. When he sees her, he also falls at the feet of the goddess. Once again, Inanna refuses to allow the *galla* to take Lulal, declaring, "He is my right arm. He is my left arm."[90]

When they enter Inanna's city of Uruk, they find Dumuzi dressed not in mourning, but in his sacred garments. Sitting on his throne and playing his reed pipe, Dumuzi is clearly relishing his power as king. As Inanna approaches him, he freezes. Realizing that he is not mourning her and that he appears unfazed by her death, Inanna becomes enraged.

Now equipped with the powers of the Great Below, "Inanna fastened on Dumuzi the eye of death."[91] Inanna declares that Dumuzi will be the one to take her place in the underworld. The *galla* seize Dumuzi and torture him. He prays to Utu, Inanna's brother, the God of the Sun and Justice. Now afraid and feeling remorse at his shortcomings, he begs his friend Utu to turn him into a snake so he can escape. Utu grants his request and Dumuzi narrowly slides away from the grasp of the *galla*.

The Dream of Dumuzi

Having just escaped the *galla* through Utu's aid, Dumuzi reverts to his normal shape and rushes to the safety of the steppe, which was his home as a young boy. Here he calls out to the familiar surroundings in an attempt to summon support from nature. He is hoping his intuitive sister hears these calls so he will be properly mourned, as he knows he is outmatched and cannot escape his fate. He lays down to sleep and plunges into a dream, from which he awakens in terror.

Dumuzi dreams that he is alone in a grove surrounded by tall, imposing trees. Before him grows a single reed that is solitary and trembling. He looks around and sees another reed, but this one has two stalks. He watches as one stalk, and then the second, disappear before his eyes. An ominous energy surrounds him. He looks next to his holy altar and sees that water has been poured over it, dampening its potency. Subsequently, he notices that his shepherd staff is missing and the churn he uses to make his precious cream and cheese has been destroyed. When he goes to his sheepfold, he watches predatory birds capture a lamb and kill a sparrow. Something has clearly maimed his sheep and goats, and he observes them fall to the earth.

Disturbed, Dumuzi awakens and immediately calls for his sister, Geshtinanna, an interpreter of dreams. Geshtinanna arrives with a close friend of Dumuzi's in tow. Geshtinanna explains that the ominous dream was a foreshadowing of the future. In it, the shepherd Dumuzi's sheepfold is "given to the winds."[92] The essence of Dumuzi and all that he represents is about to dissolve. The image of a single reed "trembling" represents, Geshtinanna tells us, Dumuzi's mother, who will mourn him. The image of a double reed represents both Geshtinanna and Dumuzi together whereby "first one, then the other, is removed,"[93] meaning they will both disappear, one after the other.

Geshtinanna explains that the destruction in Dumuzi's dream is about his own demise and, as king, the subsequent impact that his death will have on the land and his people. Once she has revealed the dream's meaning, he tells her to run immediately from the *galla* who will come in pursuit of her. Both Geshtinanna and Dumuzi's friend run away together.

Before they flee, Dumuzi commands them both to "tell no one of my hiding place."[94] The *galla* pursue Dumuzi, looking for him in the home of his sister and his friend. They go first to Geshtinanna and torture her to reveal her brother's whereabouts, but she does not give him up. It is Dumuzi's friend who ultimately betrays him for a gift of "water" and "grain" offered by the *galla*.

When the *galla* find Dumuzi, he appeals to Utu once more and pleads to be turned into a gazelle. Utu again grants his wish and Dumuzi escapes again. He hides in the house of an old woman named Belili, who takes pity on him and offers sustenance, acknowledging him as Inanna's husband. However, the *galla* have once again tracked Dumuzi to his new location, and when the old woman leaves her house, they enter.

Again, he narrowly escapes to the sheepfold of his sister. Geshtinanna begins to mourn because she can see the future and knows he will be caught. As seven *galla* descend upon him, he is surrounded and bound. Each one tortures him. "The first *galla* struck Dumuzi on the cheek with a piercing nail, / The second *galla* struck Dumuzi on the other cheek with the shepherd's crook."[95] He is stripped of his holy garments and taken naked. "Dumuzi was no more."[96]

The Return

The city of Uruk mourns the death of Dumuzi, who is to take Inanna's place in the underworld. Inanna's emotions have softened and she feels sadness at his departure. She begins to reflect on all the things that she can no longer experience with him. She moves toward her own grief. Sirtur, Dumuzi's mother, also weeps for him. Grief settles over the land.

Geshtinanna, devastated, wanders around her city, reflecting on her loss and longing to help Dumuzi. She declares, "I would share his fate."[97] Inanna finds Geshtinanna and feels the grief of her sister-in-law, which elicits an even deeper shift within. In a change of heart, Inanna wants to comfort her sister-in-law by taking her to see Dumuzi—but she does not know where he is.

Then, suddenly, a sacred fly appears. Remembering the significance the two flies had for her in the underworld, Inanna reads the sign appropriately. The fly offers to tell Inanna where Dumuzi can be found, in exchange for a gift. She makes this arrangement, gifting the fly entry to the beerhouses and taverns as a reward. Inanna and Geshtinanna follow the directions of the fly to "the edges of the steppe,"[98] where they find Dumuzi crying. Inanna declares to Dumuzi:

> You will go to the underworld,
> Half the year.
> Your sister, since she has asked,
> Will go the other half.
> On the day that you are called,
> That day you will be taken.
> On the day that Geshtinanna is called,
> That day you will be set free.[99]

Thus, Inanna decrees the fate of both Dumuzi and Geshtinanna. The masculine and feminine forces have been commanded into balance, evenly sharing the cycle of dark and light. The myth ends with Inanna surrendering Dumuzi to Spirit, resolute in her faith.

THE MYTH EXPLAINED

The Descent of Inanna (continued)

All three of these myths hinge on the heart as central to healing and evolution, highlighting the capacity for grief as a transmutative tool. In this part of Inanna's descent story, we see Dumuzi representing the wounded male. Inanna recognizes that he must evolve in order to be an effective king.

Initially, we find him excited to be atop his throne, playing his reed pipe without any cares, despite the recent death of his wife. Inanna is angered at first, but her frustration does not exceed her own heartbreak at feeling unloved by Dumuzi. Blessed with Divine vision, Inanna intuits that because he is in a position of power, this wounding could cause harm to her people. Inanna knows that a wounded male in a position of power as king would lead to imbalance among her people and her land. As High Priestess, she sets Dumuzi on his own initiatory path. She understands on a soul level the need for such a transformation.

The Dream of Dumuzi

In this powerful myth, we are reminded of the feminine association with dreams. Geshtinanna is sought to make sense of what Dumuzi cannot understand. What she sees breaks her heart but also informs her of what steps to take to help right the balance in the world. She discerns the symbolism of the reeds in his dream. As noted in the introduction "Freefall: Finding Your Bearings," a double reed post is symbolic of Inanna herself.

Also noteworthy, however, is the fact that they grow in the marshlands, that liminal space between land and water.

Geshtinanna understands that the single reed trembling in the wind represents their grieving mother, a foreshadowing of her loss of both children. Geshtinanna sees the double-stalked reed as herself and Dumuzi, where first one and then the other is taken away. Geshtinanna's courage and integrity are revealed here as she refuses to give up Dumuzi's whereabouts, highlighting her strength. She does not yield even when tortured. Dumuzi's male friend, on the other hand, is easily manipulated into disclosing Dumuzi's whereabouts when the demons offer him gifts.

Dumuzi is seized by seven demons, mirroring Inanna's process at the seven gates. The seven *galla* threaten and intimidate him. Ultimately, Dumuzi is stripped naked and brought to his death, just as Inanna was.

The Return

This myth is about the transformational power of grief and the ways in which a broken heart can lead to the heart opening. Through the experience of grief, Inanna gains access to the vulnerability of heartbreak. It is this softening and expansiveness in her heart that inspires a restoration of balance. When Inanna decrees the fate of Dumuzi to remain in the underworld half the year, while Geshtinanna goes down to take his place for the other half, she sets in motion the cycle of fertility. In Sumerian culture, Dumuzi's return becomes marked by the New Year's celebration of *hieros gamos*. The cycle of fertility is evenly split between masculine and feminine; a balance is set in motion at the hand of our heroine. The cycles of light and dark, symbolized by the periods of time spent by Geshtinanna and Dumuzi in the world above and below, establishes a cultural prioritization and honoring of the cycles of nature, both within and without.

To Dream is To Weave

According to some perspectives of dream analysis, everything in the dream is a symbol of the self. Using this framework, let us explore these three myths, to help us integrate. When Inanna hears her call to Spirit and goes to the Great Below, she comes face to face with her sister self Ereshkigal. She goes to the underworld to access that which was disavowed and unconscious. In reconciling this, she becomes whole. In facing her fears and letting go of her attachment and in purifying each of her seven energy centers, Inanna is born anew.

The knowledge—*gnosis*—she has gleaned from death and letting go, leads her to mastery, when combined together with the wisdom of the heart: the love of her grandfather Enki, the compassion Ereshkigal experienced by being witnessed by the two flies, and the kindness shown by Geshtinanna to her brother. Knowledge and the wisdom of the heart are the key aspects of Inanna's transformative process.

In showing Ereshkigal love and compassion, the Queen of the Underworld shifts from representing destruction to symbolizing transmutation. If Ereshkigal is an aspect of Inanna, the process of letting go of earthly attachments that Ereshkigal forces Inanna to do is directly connected to her liberation and transformation. Thus, these two parts of her are now working in support of each other. They have been reconciled.

Her grandfather, the God of Wisdom, is an aspect of Inanna herself— she, too, embodies wisdom. Ninshubur is like her higher self, guiding her and protecting her as devoted counsel. The fly is also symbolic. As mentioned in Gate One, the fly is the insect of death, but it is also extremely common. These insects are drawn to decay, the counterpart of renewal. The presence of the fly highlights that in grief, there is an opportunity for renewal. Renewal is accomplished through the efforts of the fly to reunite

Inanna and her sister-in-law with Dumuzi. Its presence underscores that death is not an end but an opportunity to renew, to evolve. Indeed, Inanna is ultimately teaching us that death is but a transition and is not to be feared. Death is the gateway to another experience of the soul.

In the story, Inanna facilitates Dumuzi's own initiation, leading him to his growth. However, if we imagine Dumuzi to be an aspect of Inanna herself, we can see him as her yang or Divine Masculine—the wounded male energy that she is ready to heal. Nevertheless, relationships are mirrors. Her beloved, the masculine, fails her.

Inanna is angry when she discovers him lost in his egoic attachment to power. This presentation of Dumuzi might represent her own tendency to be pulled toward ego. Upon this realization—consciously or unconsciously— she fixes the eye of death upon him.

In Dumuzi's focus on self, Inanna is reminded of the seduction of power— realizing that she has just acquired even more power through her descent and ascent. Selecting Dumuzi as her replacement in the underworld can also be read as Inanna's attempt to protect her own ego from the potential of using her newly acquired power in a self-aggrandizing way. This decision, then, is one that is meant to bring her further into balance.

The Backstory

Geshtinanna is a devoted sister. Inanna recognizes Geshtinanna's courage and compassion, which leads her to decree Geshtinanna's fate of splitting the year in the underworld with her brother. This decision brings Ereshkigal and Inanna even closer. Through this decision, Inanna ensures Ereshkigal always has companionship. It can also be seen as Inanna's prioritization of the embodiment of both masculine and feminine forces—her own androgyny demonstrates an evenly-balanced combination of masculine and feminine.

Indeed, Inanna and Ereshkigal have, on some level, united and become one. This unity is made accessible by Inanna's ability to reconcile the shadow and Ereshkigal's capacity to receive love and compassion. Each goddess successfully actualizes that which is most necessary for their individual healing, and this draws them into wholeness, whereby they merge. If Ereshkigal is an aspect of Inanna—her sister self—then Inanna is present both above and below.

When we first meet Ereshkigal, she is a solitary widow. The back story first mentioned in Gate One comes from the Akkadian myth *The Epic of Gilgamesh*.[100] In that myth, Gilgamesh is the one who ultimately slays Ereshkigal's husband Gugalanna, who is also called the Bull of Heaven—but it is actually Inanna who instigates the process.

In *The Epic of Gilgamesh*, Inanna comes across the handsome hero Gilgamesh, who has returned from an expedition in which he and his friend Enkidu have killed the monstrous Huwawa—a demon who guarded the cedar forest. Finding Gilgamesh freshly bathed after his journey, his hair loose down his back, full of swagger and radiating confidence, she is filled with desire and proposes that he become her lover.

But Gilgamesh scorns the goddess. He refuses her advance by detailing the fates of her lovers past who, like Dumuzi, were all in some way put to death. He will not risk meeting a similar fate. He refuses her allure. Angered by this, Inanna asks the Sky God An to unleash the Bull of Heaven on Gilgamesh, because "Gilgamesh has recounted my stinking deeds, my stench and my foulness."[101] The God An reluctantly agrees.

Inanna brings down the Bull of Heaven, Gugalanna, and lets him loose. Destruction ensues and it takes both Gilgamesh and his friend Enkidu together to fight against him. Gugalanna is taken down by a sword

"Between neck and horns."[102] Ultimately, the two kill the Bull of Heaven and tear out his heart. When Inanna curses them, Enkidu rips off Gugalanna's right thigh and throws it at her. Inanna then sets up a lament over his right thigh to honor him.

In *The Return*, Inanna's decision for her replacement in the underworld ensures that Ereshkigal will not be solitary. In effect, she shares her husband and her sister-in-law with Ereshkigal, balancing her karmic debt and ensuring Ereshkigal has companionship in the underworld all year round.

To Everything There is a Season

Significantly, Inanna restores balance to the Earth plane where the destruction of the Divine Feminine was underway at the hand of the wounded male. Indeed, Dumuzi's glorification of his power and complete lack of respect or mourning for his wife foreshadows the shift in goddess cultures that is to come. Threatened by its potency, the patriarchy will usurp the Divine Feminine. Prophetic Inanna attempts to forestall this demise by commanding a process of transformation for the wounded male, as symbolized by her husband, to become whole and healed. This in turn restores balance to the Earth plane by way of creating the seasons.

It is noteworthy that there is confusion among scholars around the timing of Dumuzi's return. I follow Samuel Noah Kramer's interpretation that Dumuzi returns to the world above in the fall. To those in the western world, this may seem counterintuitive given that in the west, generally crops mature and must be harvested or they begin to die as we approach winter. In ancient Sumer, however, two seasons evenly split the year marked by the two equinoxes. Dumuzi descends to the Great Below at the spring equinox and remains there during the heat of summer. He returns to his wife at the autumnal equinox, which was the New Year in Sumer. During this return, the sacred sexual union between the two leads to the regrowth of the crops.[103]

The initiation and transformation Inanna goes through in her descent and subsequent ascent makes her capable of rebalancing the Earth and bringing fertility to the land, through her own transformation. The journey always begins within. If you understand your initiation through the descent and subsequent ascent as the journey of the unapologetic heroine, then you might feel a strong resonance with Inanna. If so, you may wish to continue working with her energy to further your process.

INTERSECTION: UNDERSTANDING OUR OWN CHALLENGES THROUGH THE GODDESS OF LOVE

Surrendering to Ascend

Ultimately, the transformation that occurs in Inanna at the end of *The Return* is inspired by the compassion demonstrated in Geshtinanna for her brother. Inanna's heart literally transforms through the power of her sister-in-law's love for her brother and the grief that settles over the land. Grief has a way of leveling our defense mechanisms and creating an opening for vulnerability. This vulnerability elicits a surrender in Inanna.

Upon the completion of an initiation, we must surrender even further in order to successfully integrate the gifts accessed from the process. In other words, after receiving the teaching from an initiation, Spirit will invite us to put it into practice. Once we do, we are fully ready and equipped for the next level of our process.

Initiations enhance us. Our world begins to reflect this change back to us. We can either resist what comes at us, or we can surrender even further, with the knowledge that what is showing up will help us anchor in the teachings of our initiation.

In the myths above, Inanna leaves the underworld equipped with the experience of her own death, which then informs her actions, even granting her the capacity to fix the eye of death upon another—as she does figuratively with Dumuzi. This capacity is not her ability to execute another; she has long held that power as the Goddess of War. Instead, this is about her newly acquired mastery of the Death Mysteries. Inanna now officially holds the secret teachings of death—her ultimate goal in descending to the underworld.

This experience grants her access to yet another role, that of midwife to the dying. She has made known the unknown journey of death and, as such, can offer clarity to those readying for such a transition. We might think of this process like those recounted by modern-day individuals who have had near-death experiences—who have died and then returned from the other side with stories and understanding that can help shift our death-phobic culture. Who knows more about death than one who has gone through it?

As a guide to ascension, Inanna is also a teacher of transition, offering an invitation to embrace our evolution and the constant movement in our spiral of growth. Inanna knows that she cannot escape the demons who walk beside her as she leaves the Great Below. She accepts the circumstance and integrates her gifts of compassion for self and other; her humility; and the equanimity that comes from balancing our karma to move forward and rise.

By fully releasing into the experience of death, Inanna let go of what was no longer in alignment—her old self. In searching for her deepest truth, she reclaimed her wholeness. In the beginning of *The Descent of Inanna*, Inanna willingly goes toward her death equipped with the faith that she will transcend it. At each gate, when she is asked to give up an item, she initially questions but ultimately yields. When she approaches Ereshkigal's throne, she is turned into a corpse. Unsure exactly how things will unfold, she does know she is powerful enough to find her way back from the Great Below with deeper understanding. She is the high priestess, being initiated as a teacher of ascension. She knows she is ready and that this is part of her destiny.

When she is returned to life and the demons come to walk alongside her, she realizes someone must take her place if she ascends. She knows balance must be maintained, and by orchestrating the balance between brother and sister representing the Divine Masculine and Divine Feminine, Inanna integrates and actualizes what she has learned.

Your Heart Directs Your Life

Inanna's ascension depends on a transformation of her heart center, enabling a kind of upgrade through which she restores balance. This is a profound teaching for what is possible for us as humans in our evolutionary process. According to the HeartMath Institute—a not-for-profit research organization and leader in emotional physiology research, techniques, and technology—the heart is even more magnetic than the brain.[104] The heart is where our beliefs reside. It is where we *feel* our feelings and where our assumptions originate.

In other words, that which is contained in the heart—one's emotional inner experience—informs the heart's magnetic field. This has a direct impact on the world around us. Love is a central tenet of most major religions and is accessed by the heart chakra. The field of neurocardiology demonstrates that the heart has neurons, like the brain.

Using the heart with intention to positively impact our reality creates a personal key code to peace, balance, and unity, made accessible to each of us through our own physiology. When we bring intention and consciousness to what is in our heart, we enhance our creative capacity and our ability to call forth that which is in alignment with the highest good, thereby connecting us to our Divinity.

As Within, So Without

Upgrading our relationship to our bodies begins with the heart. As a clinical psychotherapist, I have consistently observed that the experience of trauma can directly impact our beliefs and, therefore, what we assume will show up in our life, sometimes in an erroneous manner. The mind attempts to make sense of trauma, because trauma leads to cognitive dissonance; we often consciously or unconsciously misalign that drive for sense-making, linking the trauma with erroneous beliefs.

For example, if someone experiences a sexual violation, they may find a way to blame the self because the act of sexual violence against them makes no sense. The ego insists on some kind of reason. The individual may then connect to a false belief that he or she caused the violence in some way, such as by leading the person on. While this is of course completely inaccurate, the feeling that it was one's fault can lead to an erroneous belief of somehow deserving the violation. As a result, they may now feel tainted, reinforcing a negative psychic narrative.

In part, this is due to a physiological shift that occurs in the brain when trauma is experienced. In his seminal book *The Body Keeps the Score: Brain, Mind, and Body in the Healing of Trauma*, renowned trauma specialist Bessel Van Der Kolk highlights, as the title implies, that trauma leaves its mark in the body. He explains, "Trauma results in a fundamental reorganization of the way the mind and brain manage perceptions. It changes not only how we think and what we think about, but also our capacity to think."[105]

The heart, as the most magnetic aspect of the body, programs the individual's field of reality. It begins to call in circumstances that mirror the beliefs we hold, whether we are conscious of those beliefs or not. This reflects the Hermetic law of "As above so below," or more specifically "As within, so without." What is in our heart is what shows up in our reality.

This gate is an opportunity to get clear about what your heart is holding—the frequency at which it is vibrating. Inanna's reality transformed as she went through her own process of surrender. She surrendered to the power of the heart in order to rise, and her example offers us inspiration and a model for our own journey.

HEALING INTERVENTION

The process of surrendering to ascend relies on the wisdom of the heart and is linked to the fourth chakra—the heart chakra. This energy center is the source of unconditional love, compassion, non-judgment, and the capacity to create the life we came here to live. Because the heart is the main informer of your reality, you must intentionally upgrade that which is no longer resonant, to support the movement toward ascension.

Begin your spiritual upgrade by assessing your readiness to change your beliefs. In doing so, you ensure that when you come to each gate of your descent, you will understand the teaching present therein with clarity and ease. Upgrading the heart can be done through ritual. Below is an invitation to release the outdated programs of the heart and install new, higher vibrational ones.

Ritual for Upgrading Outdated Beliefs

Items required: Two pieces of paper, a pen, fire pit or fireplace, altar, or green space. State the following prayer:

> May Inanna come forward to help me upgrade any outdated beliefs that I am ready to shift in this now moment.

STEP 1. Surround yourself in light or simply say: The Light protects me. Imagine that you have roots emerging from your feet, much like from a tree, anchoring you into the Earth's core so you are fully grounded.

STEP 2. Call in the high-level beings with whom you are connected and with whom you resonate. This can be Inanna, the ascended masters, angels, guides, loved ones, Source, God, Goddess, the All That Is—whatever feels most aligned with you. Ask for their Divine assistance in transmuting your old beliefs to upgrade them such that they are in full alignment with your highest good and healing.

STEP 3. Sit in meditation and ask for clarity about what you are ready to release and upgrade. Write up a list of these outdated beliefs on the first paper. For example, perhaps you have an outdated belief that it is unsafe for you to be who you are. You might think the following:

> I believe that the world is an unsafe place for me to be who I truly am, and that when I share my true gifts with the world I will be ridiculed, judged, or vilified. I believe that when I am truly myself, stand in my power, and allow myself to be

seen as I really am, I get hurt—because the world is out to get me and is a dangerous place for me.

STEP 4. Sit in meditation and ask for guidance on upgrading the list. Drop your consciousness into your heart center and listen. Do this by bringing your hand to you heart so you can feel the contact and imagine you are perceiving from the location where your hand rests. What comes up? Write down the upgraded version on the second piece of paper. For example, the antidote to the outdated belief that it is unsafe for you to be who you are might be the following:

> The world is a safe place for me to be who I truly am. When I share my gifts with the world, I am respected, celebrated, and met with support and love. When I am fully witnessed standing in my power, the Universe helps me carry out my unique mission here on Earth, so I experience fulfillment on every level.

STEP 5. Take the first paper, with the erroneous list, and burn it in the fireplace or fire pit. When doing so, ask your guides to ensure that everything you are burning in your fire is fully transmuted into love. You may also simply state: These old, outdated, erroneous beliefs are being fully transmuted into love, in alignment with my highest good and healing and the highest good and healing of all.

STEP 6. Take the second piece of paper, with the upgraded list. If you are doing this outside, put your list on the ground and gather some dirt in your hands. Cover your upgraded list with the dirt. Alternatively, if doing this at your altar, use your imagination to see yourself placing dirt over your list on the bare earth. Looking down at it, close your eyes and imagine this dirt is like your garden and the items on your list are the seeds you have just planted. Your list is now figuratively ready to take root.

If you are outside, once you have completed the imagery you may pick up your paper, leaving the dirt on the ground in that spot. This will serve to continue to hold the energy there of what you have planted to grow. If you are doing it at your altar, read it aloud with authority. Then hold the paper to your own heart, to be transmitted directly into your heart center through energetic osmosis, thereby directly upgrading the old, outmoded thoughts in your heart itself. Place the paper folded on your altar under your favorite talisman (a crystal, stone, feather, etc.), and light a candle. Keep it lit for a short while as an honoring, and to give it the energy of action.

STEP 7. Give thanks to the beings that you called upon for help. Here, you might put an offering on your altar for them, such as a few drops of essential oil, a few pieces of sage or sweet grass, or even simply a hand-drawn image of a heart. Choose whatever inspires you; the intention of gratitude is enough. Finally end by saying: It is done. It is done. It is done.

STEP 8. Release the elements, the directions, and all the beings you called in for assistance. Now brace yourself, as ritual works quickly. Expect that the shift is complete and proceed in alignment with this truth. Pay attention to situations that may trigger you and elicit the old tendencies, and notice how quickly your new upgrade intercepts and prevents this from happening. It gets increasingly stronger through every opportunity in which you are triggered and are still able to stand firm.

As in Cognitive Behavioral Therapy (CBT), a new way of thinking gets laid down through the upgrade. You behave differently because you expect and believe in a different outcome, and your emotions or feelings reflect your new way of thinking. You begin to cope with life from an empowered perspective. You are beginning to walk alongside Inanna in all her high priestess energy. You now share her lineage of heart-centered wisdom.

A Return to Your Story

Mantra to support process:

> I embody the wisdom of the heart and rise unapologetically
> as the heroine I am.

Go back to your journal that you began in Gate One, where you rewrote your story as the heroine. Read it through and then start a new page. Here, write about your own ascent, your *happily ever after* wildest dream. Imagine that you are healed, transformed, and resurrected as a fully initiated heroine. Specify what is in your heart. Script your vision of what is possible. Visualize and *feel* that reality with the help of Inanna. Use her story to guide you. Remember that as she ascended to the world above, everything in the above, within, and below was adjusted simultaneously.

What does your adjustment look like, so you may experience fulfillment on every level, as Inanna did? By thinking about and articulating these adjustments, you facilitate their manifestation. Things will radically transform in your life when you reframe your journey as an initiation of the unapologetic heroine.

You may wish to begin your fresh page with the following prompts:

> Now that I have been born anew, I am ready to ....
> I commit to carrying out my heart's desire to...
> My vision of what the future looks like for me is...

My relationships reflect my transformation by...

I express myself creatively and with confidence through...

My true purpose and my work in the world align to...

I positively influence the world by...

I celebrate and revel in...

When done, read all you have written and let yourself be inspired by you!

Through this gate, you, like Inanna, have practiced the art of surrender, the ability to let go and enter a state of acceptance. This allowed you to upgrade your heart to ensure your beliefs are where you wish them to be. Your upgrade is a significant aspect of ascension. It positions you to ensure that the ever-evolving chapters you write next accurately reflect the wisdom of your heart.

There is a difference between this wisdom and knowledge. Many individuals who hold an enormous amount of authority have knowledge. By contrast, Inanna emerges as one who has knowledge while also prioritizing the wisdom of the heart—our inner wisdom. With the heart center activated and healed, you are able to embody your Divine nature. Inanna has taken you through her own journey.

Ultimately, as souls, we individuated from Source to experience our own creative ability; part of the creative process in which we are engaged is determining how to return to Source. Indeed, the Goddess of Love shows us that it always comes back to love. Love is, and always has been, the way.

Next, we will explore how to take the gifts from this journey with Inanna and emulate her in creating Heaven on Earth. Through integrating what has unfolded, blossomed, and elevated within you, you have all that is necessary to take the next steps in your training to become a present-day priest/ess of Inanna, if you so choose. You will learn how to actualize your role as an unapologetic teacher of the wisdom of the heart.

Next Steps for the Present-Day Priest/ess of Inanna

Having gone through each gate has helped re-establish your connection to Inanna. You are now being invited to work with her more closely to join the wider collective of lightworkers pursuing this same path. As a united front, your impact will be astronomical. While priest/ess training is a formal and highly involved, holy commitment, you might consider this an invitation to prepare to train more deeply so that one day you can join the Order of Inanna as her present-day priest/ess.

By aligning your intention and attention to this pursuit, you become proficient at bringing Inanna's wisdom into the world and positively shifting your own life while raising the collective vibration of the universe. The following concepts will help you further integrate the work you have already done, to ensure you feel fully equipped and confident in your ability to have an exponential impact. And remember, everything in the life of a priest/ess reflects the priest/ess path. Everything. The events of your life are by design. Accordingly, you cannot ignore the inner messages that direct you to step fully into the life you came here to live—to link arms with your cosmic team of lightworkers and actualize the change you came here to create.

SHINE ON, SISTER, SHINE ON

One of the things that sets Inanna apart is her unapologetic nature. She is unafraid to own her mastery. She knows she is a force, and she celebrates her power, demonstrating it with ease. She inhabits her role as guide with confidence. This is why we need her today.

Every one of you reading this is a master in your own right and possesses the ability to ascend, just as Inanna does. Although she is a goddess, she represents the same polarities that exist in each of you, and, as such, she is no different from you. She is here to encourage you to own your mastery, to move into the role of guide, to teach, to serve, to uplift, to unite, to transform and rebalance the Earth from a vantage point of love.

Endowed with the skills, tools, and gifts you have received through your individual experience at each gate, Inanna is now ushering you to the platform most aligned with your frequency, to share this wisdom by being the guide you are. Inanna is a teacher of teachers on the path of ascension. She has helped you remember that you are also a teacher— someone who has come into this life specifically to help lead humanity toward higher consciousness.

To that end, I outline the next steps needed to promote the integration of the work you've done with Inanna thus far and to advance your role as a lightworker. Inanna reminds you there is nothing egotistical about owning your mastery and seeing yourself through the lens of the Divine. Instead, she helps you access the grace that a true teacher embodies: the confidence in your own authority even while exhibiting humility.

THREE SACRED CONCEPTS FOR INTEGRATION

Incorporating the following three sacred concepts will support your process of integrating the journey you have just taken with Inanna. These concepts help develop the confidence and Divine clarity that allows you to sync up with your cosmic team as a teacher of the wisdom of the heart. Characteristic of all Inanna's medicine, these sacred concepts are in service of all. This is the power of unity consciousness.

The three sacred concepts include: the ability to drop all inner and outer judgment; the capacity to work with the spiritual principal of grace; and the ability to deepen your understanding of the Death Mysteries by learning how to live fully and take care of your unfinished business.

DROPPING INNER AND OUTER JUDGMENT

Inanna is a brilliant teacher of nonjudgment. She follows her heart unapologetically, without second-guessing or invalidating herself. Many of you on the spiritual path may struggle with being a teacher or claiming your capability as a guide, for fear that doing so lacks humility. There is nothing egotistical about shining as brightly as you came here to shine. You do stand out and you are a catalyst. You create a stir because you were meant to.

When doubt surfaces on the path of your own evolution—and it will—it is an opportunity to engage with it as a part of your training. Can you continue to stand in your authority even when insecurity surfaces and leads you to judge yourself? Accomplishing this is part of the path of mastery. Overcoming the inner tendency to judge self or others is a necessary aspect of being a teacher of the heart.

As the Goddess of Love, Inanna consistently alchemizes lower vibrational frequency to support evolution. Recall the experience she had with her grandfather Enki in the myth *Inanna and the God of Wisdom*, which we explored in Gate Two: "Healing Ancestral Relationships." Enki drunkenly gifted Inanna the *me*—the spiritual powers of the land and the laws of civilization. Then, after Enki sobered up, he realized what he had done and he wanted them all back. He unleashed monsters on her.

Yet Inanna did not judge him. Instead, she used her mastery to transform the situation into one that served all. In the end, her people received the *me*. Inanna's wise servant and counselor, Ninshubur, had the opportunity to prove herself as an important exemplar of a female heroine who is a strong protector and defender—a shaman in her own right.

In the end of the myth, Enki arrives at the celebration, having realized how deserving of the *me* Inanna is. This results in manifesting even more *me*. Inanna's efforts and non-judgment foster Enki's successful movement through his wounding around the misuse of power. Inanna handles her role as a catalyst with the integrity and skill that comes from a high-vibration perspective.

Because we have an ego on the Earth plane, it is natural that an inclination to judge self or others may arise. What matters is what we do with that inclination. Even if such judgments surface about someone else, we can approach these feelings as an invitation to transmute that judgment, so it becomes a guide into our unresolved matters within. Judgment is a lot like projection—at its core, it is really an inner judgment. If we follow the thread that leads us to our own issues instead of getting caught up in judging others, we can work through it and bring light to the shadow, inevitably moving us into compassion.

When we are successful, we let go of judgment and it becomes instantly transformed in the akashic field, bringing us one step closer to our mastery.

The akashic field is where our akashic records are stored— our unique energetic file in the cosmic cloud of all that we are. It is the constantly updated consciousness of our soul, which includes the entirety of our experiences, actions, thoughts, words, and intentions.

COMPASSION DISSOLVES JUDGMENT

If we read judgment that surfaces in us as a signpost, alerting us to look for the thread back to our inner selves, we will be able to unpack the issue and, as we do, the judgment begins to dissolve. We then develop compassion for the very thing we were judging. We cannot hold compassion and judgment in the heart at the same time.

As we saw in the descent and ascent of Inanna, compassion is a key in transformation and rebirth. In addition, we can shift the energy of judgment into energy of action and begin to come into congruence with the issue that is at its root. Inanna acts with immediacy; she recognizes what needs to be done and simply goes toward it without fear. Borrow this capacity of hers. Try it out and see how she can inspire you.

When you live embodying the wisdom of Inanna, the Goddess of Love, you make your heart *the* directional signal—the GPS for all aspects of your life, as it were. By choosing to live according to heart-centered intention in every action, thought, word, and feeling experienced, you inspire others to positively uplift the vibration of the entire planet.

Let judgment be the vehicle through which you learn how to heal your own dissonance and actively transform it into compassion, freeing yourself for the last time from its limiting and destructive nature. Do so at every opportunity, so you can teach others how to do the same. As you stand in your role as a guide and you become more visible, have a larger reach, and command more attention, you will reflect what a heart without judgment looks like.

ALIGNING WITH GRACE

Grace shows up in many aspects of the spiritual path and is a central tenet of ascension, or the progression into a new paradigm of love and unity. Grace is a spiritual law which, at its core, is about allowing what is aligned with the highest good to unfold without resistance. When we intentionally and consciously work with the principal of grace, we merge with its power and become instruments through which grace is manifested in the world.

In other words, as teachers of the wisdom of the heart, engaging the principal of grace is essential. By doing so, we ensure that what we bring forward is aligned only with highest good. In her role as a goddess of justice, Inanna uses the Law of Grace to bring about justice that serves all.

In Gate Six, "Transcending the Binary," we explored Inanna's capacity to consecrate an individual's identity to match their heart. Inanna's energy works like a bridge to link us to our most holy and authentic expression, allowing grace to support our evolution. Grace is like an entry point to the energy of flow, and when we engage grace, our experiences are carried in the current of Divine ease.

When we lean into grace, we learn to accept and grow without resistance, even during the process of clearing our karma. Understanding karmic balancing is a central tenet of the path of the priest/ess. Karma is the law of cause and effect and a governing principle of life. In *The Tibetan Book of Living and Dying*, Sogyal Rinpoche explains, "The word karma literally means 'action,' and karma is both the power latent within actions, and the results our actions bring."[106] When we understand how karma works and why, we begin to act accordingly, fully aware that everything we do has an impact on everything around us. With that understanding, we live consciously.

When we put out love and kindness, it comes back to us tenfold. Similarly, when we put out anything that is of a lower vibration, that also comes back to us tenfold. It is not a punishment. Understanding this allows us to grow and evolve—to better understand our own capacity as a Divine creator.

Chances are, if you are reading this book, you came to this incarnation with the intention to clear as much karma as you can in this lifetime. If so, it is because your higher self understands that to balance karma is a necessary part of your soul's transcendence. If this is your current process, you may have experienced what feels like great suffering, particularly early on in your life. I invite you to reframe this suffering through the lens of karmic healing and engage grace to help you integrate your process from a place of empowerment. When we are able to access grace in balancing our karma, is it successfully reconciled and we can begin to move toward an evolutionary path that works without resistance. This is a path wherein the choices we make are aligned with the highest vibrational frequency. Grace shifts us toward growth with ease instead of challenge.

To inhabit this new model of high vibrational ease, we must ensure we are untethered from the past so we can move forward. Using the ability to transform judgment into compassion and engaging the power of grace, we can deepen our understanding of the Death Mysteries—the wisdom teachings Inanna sought to come into her wholeness. Inanna understood the wisdom of the Death Mysteries as teachings about how to live consciously in the now, and how through presence and non-attachment we can take steps in our life that are aligned with our destiny as written by our higher self.

In practicing acceptance of the continuous change that is life, we learn how to *allow* instead of resist. These teachings highlight the importance of taking care of our unfinished business to access a felt sense of liberation and presence. This feeling is necessary to live in an embodied state of love, unity, and peace.

TAKING CARE OF YOUR UNFINISHED BUSINESS

Inanna is a teacher of death. Per the myths, she is most well known for her own death—and that is no doubt by design. She commands our attention to the significance of the Death Mysteries as a wise teaching for how to live in a way that readies us for our own ascension.

For Inanna, death is all about life. The process of surrender and the courage to face our fear grants us the capacity to be born anew into our most powerful version of ourselves. Inanna is not afraid of death because she knows that everything is always in transition. She understands death as a part of her transcendence. She makes known all parts of herself so she can be free to ascend.

Take a moment to assess if there are any areas in your emotional landscape that feel particularly out of sync with where you are now. You have made many upgrades in your work with Inanna. When exploring the ground of your emotional world, are there any sections of your personal garden that you feel you have left unattended? Has this particular garden bed dried up? In end-of-life work, this is what we would call our "unfinished business."

USING THE DEATH MYSTERIES FOR THE ART OF LIVING

As a hospice social worker, I sat with many people as they took their last breath. In witnessing the differences between various deaths, I was able to see how an individual's unfinished business impacted the active dying process. I recall the example of one elderly man in particular. Let's call him Robert.

Hospice does an amazing job at identifying when an individual commences the active dying process, often enabling family to arrange to be present. In this case, I had been working with Robert, as well as with his family, for several weeks. His adult children were estranged from him. They had come to sign paperwork because he was not able to do so himself.

When I met with the family, they explained that their father had been abusive, sexually and physically. The adult children had no intention of forgiving their father; they made this clear. They expressed that they did not want to be present for his death. They signed the paperwork and returned home, explaining that they would not be coming back.

Arrangements had already been made with the local funeral home and their presence was no longer needed. The patient had end-stage dementia, so he was not able to do any process-oriented therapy.

The medical director of the amazing hospice where I worked was open-minded and allowed social workers to provide Reiki—as long as there was consent by the healthcare proxy and if the patient was unable to engage in talk therapy. So I provided Reiki during Robert's active dying process. It was a very lengthy and distressed experience, quite unlike all others I had witnessed. He had no family present and, other than the hospice team, the only folks ever in his room were the nursing home staff. There were no personal belongings in the room—nothing to offset the blankness of the facility.

It is common for family to bring in items that reflect the patient's personality, objects that help them feel more at home and spark passion: a familiar comforter, photos of loved ones, favorite music, memorabilia of their life, guitars, fishing rods, and anything else that feels personal. This room had nothing but an empty tray table pushed against the wall, an empty chair, and blank walls. Even the shades were drawn, blocking out the soft fall sunlight.

A WINDOW INTO THE UNRESOLVED

When we leave our business unfinished, it impacts the ease and flow of what is possible and creates a physical, emotional, spiritual, and mental log jam that makes accessing equanimity challenging. As a hospice team, we had concluded that Robert's family would likely experience what is referred to as a complicated bereavement process, given the unfinished business surrounding the abuse.

Knowing that no family members were going to be present, we had hospice volunteers join the team to sit with him and support him. I covered the gaps in the schedule.

While every individual is different, the active dying process usually lasts around three days. In Robert's case, several more days slipped by while he appeared to struggle with his release. It was almost a full week of him presenting with what is called Cheyne-Stokes breathing, varying from very deep breathing to no breathing at all. He also experienced hallucinations, agitation, delirium, an inability to close his eyes, a high heart rate, and low blood pressure.

Robert also moaned loudly throughout most of this time. While sounds can occur in the vocal cords during the dying process as the person approaches expiration, his moaning was accompanied by distinct grimacing. His physical pain was being well-managed by the hospice nurses, but he was clearly in psychic pain, and the entire team could see that. It was apparent to each of us that he was struggling with his unfinished business.

As his throat constricted around each slow inhalation, it was hard not to imagine it as a psychic moan echoing across all that was left unsaid in his family dynamic. We cannot outrun our past. We must make peace with it.

A PEACEFUL EXIT

Alternatively, I worked with someone in hospice who was actively taking care of her unfinished business during our time together. Let's call her Mary. She made this work a part of her daily practice while in hospice. Hers was a death that moved me to awe. In her death, I saw a courage and equanimity I had never before witnessed.

Still, to this day, her powerful process stands out as an example of what is possible. I will always remember her as my greatest teacher of alchemical transition. She not only accepted her death, but she was able to negotiate her conscious preparation for the journey she was about to take, while also staying present—her feet rooted firmly to the Earth for the time her body allowed. With a short life expectancy because her breast cancer had metastasized into her bones, she continued to eat only the food allowed in her macrobiotic diet. She did so through her very last day.

In deep acceptance of her impending transition, Mary still felt that a macrobiotic diet was a way to bring more light into her cancer-ravaged body. She believed that it would be easier to release herself from a light-filled body. She was profoundly courageous.

ACTIVE LETTING GO

Mary had identified to me that letting go of some of her material attachments was part of her unfinished business. Throughout her fifty-six years, she had collected beautiful pieces of art in the form of jewelry from all around the world. In fact, the closet where she housed the pieces looked like an art museum. She made it a priority to give away every single piece of that collection as a gesture toward release, much as Inanna gave up her earthly possessions when she went through her descent into the underworld.

Shortly before Mary's death, I came to her home for our usual session. I was wearing tan dress pants and a black T-shirt under a turquoise cardigan. As I entered her bedroom—where she sat, diminutive, in the middle of her king-sized bed—she seemed to study me. As I pulled the chair closer to her bed, she said, "Wait, I have something I have to give you."

She got up and walked to her closet. It was painful for me to watch because she was in so much discomfort, and it took her a solid five minutes to walk a few feet. But she emerged from her closet with something and placed it over my neck, saying, "This necklace matches your outfit perfectly." It was an unusual and exquisite turquoise necklace made of Czechoslovakian glass.

I told her that I couldn't take it, but she insisted, stating that it was part of her practice of taking care of her unfinished business. I graciously took it, knowing that I would later give it back to her family because as a social worker, I was not allowed to accept any gifts. But in service of her process of taking care of her unfinished business, I accepted it in the moment, moved beyond words.

Her family would not let me return it. Today, I wear it at any time I need courage, and always I think of her. The jewelry symbolizes an ongoing teaching in gracefully letting go and taking care of whatever is unfinished.

GLIDING THROUGH THE MAJESTIC PORTAL

When Mary entered her active dying process, not only was she fully prepared, but it was one of the most beautiful deaths I have ever witnessed. She was free of pain and peaceful, and the air in her room was filled with sacred energy. Her daughter read aloud from the *Tibetan Book of the Dead* as she had requested, to help guide her soul through the death process consciously. There was a sense of celebration, calmness, open-heartedness, and joy in her room.

Mary was indeed an unapologetic heroine full of grace and courage, even in the face of her own death. Her capacity to make peace with her life, herself, and all that was unfinished led to her felt sense of liberation as she seemed to float easily through her transition.

TAKE ACTION NOW

As midwife to the death process, Inanna teaches us that engaging in life as a preparation for our own great transition becomes a skillful approach to living our life. There is no need to wait until you are making the transition from this life to the next to take care of your unfinished business. Do it now and keep it current. When you do, you will feel lightness in your heart.

In the AA model, this might look somewhat like Steps Eight and Nine, in which you make amends—but this is not just about relationships with others. Taking care of unfinished business is primarily about our relationship to ourselves, just as Inanna's teachings highlight. In this way, you can address what you might want to give up or shift so that you may step more fully into the self-acceptance that allows you to live unapologetically and at your highest vibration. It is about being honest with yourself and being willing to always look within to ensure you *live* consciously.

GET REALLY HONEST WITH YOURSELF

This is not a path of rules. It is open, inclusive, and flowing. It is a path that is unique for every individual. Honor what feels right and aligned for you. Perhaps there is simply a gear shift being welcomed in, so that your relationship to whatever you do can sync up with your current rhythm. If your intuition is urging you to bring healing or resolution to relationships with others, or with yourself; to start working out or to work out less; to try a sport or activity you have always wanted to try; to eat a particular way; to incorporate meditation; to take an extended time off work; to go away on a vacation or adventure alone; to go back to school; to get a new certification; to stop attending school; to have a baby; to launch a business; or to express yourself creatively—do it now. There is no better time, and it will help you come even more fully into congruence.

Borrow some of Inanna's spontaneous, unbridled immediacy and take care of your unfinished business. Very often, when you return to walk this path with conscious intention, whatever is out of alignment surfaces. You will know what this is and, with courage, you will be able to make the adjustments your higher self is urging. Ask Inanna to guide you.

YOU HAVE THE POWER

As a teacher of ascension, Inanna has come back to help you in your individual process, while we all move as a collective toward this end. As the Goddess of Love, she is directing us to the new reality we are joining together to weave, and that reality is one of love. This was always her mission, and this is her time.

It is also your time. Inanna wants you to remember your own power. Align your heart with hers through intention and allow your life to become a magical process by which you see your mastery. Inanna cannot violate your free will, so you have to ask for her help. You have to collaborate willingly. Take her hand and open your heart to her. Her devoted worshipper and advocate, the poet Enheduanna, reminds us how equipped Inanna is to be our guide. She is capable of clearing our unique path and helping us find our footing through the unknown terrain. She writes of our heroine:

> to smooth the traveler's road
> to clear a path for the weak
> are yours Inanna
>
> to straighten the footpath
> to make firm the cleft place
> are yours Inanna
>
> to destroy to build
> to lift up to put down
> are yours Inanna
>
> to turn man into woman
> woman into man
> are yours Inanna[107]

Here, Enheduanna highlights Inanna's ability to sanctify your path and ceremoniously alchemize your life to sync up with your heart; to help you release what no longer serves you; and to help you construct a life that matches the pure, unconditional love of unity consciousness.

Take in all that she has to offer you now. You are ready. You have been initiated through her wisdom. If you decide to continue to work with

Inanna, she will show up for you in the most amazing and supportive ways. She will help you to live in congruence within and without.

Go forward now in your journey with confidence. Own your mastery. Share your gifts and wisdom with world. Carry out the mission you came here to actualize. Be the love you wish to see.

May Inanna speak directly to you and help you live unapologetically true to yourself, and may *you* help others do the same.

Appendix

PORTAL	GUIDANCE	CHAKRA
Gate One	Heeding a call to Spirit as an initiation to develop the faith that allows you to view your path from a place of empowerment.	**Crown Chakra**
Gate Two	Healing ancestral relationships so you may reclaim your authentic voice and ensure you only perpetuate and communicate the gifts from your ancestral line.	**Throat Chakra**
Gate Three	Transcending fear by releasing attachments and addictive tendencies that keep us bound. Learning how to let go and let goddess.	**Solar Plexus Chakra**
Gate Four	Reclaiming a positive sense of self and relationship to your sexuality, creativity, and appetites by transmuting lingering wounding held within the sacral chakra, to experience joy.	**Sacral Chakra**
Gate Five	Accessing a felt sense of safety and groundedness by erecting sacred boundaries.	**Root Chakra**
Gate Six	Developing the discernment to see yourself with clarity, to step beyond the binary and all perceived limitations so you may honor your unique truth and live in congruence within and without.	**Third Eye Chakra**
Gate Seven	Becoming conscious that the heart is the directional center of your being. Updating erroneous beliefs held in the heart to magnetize a high vibration reality.	**Heart Chakra**

161

NOTE ON THE CHAKRA CHART

The classification of the chakra system as numerically ordered and linked developmentally according to a particular chronology is useful; however, given the simultaneity of our soul-level experience in space and time, such a classification presents a challenge. Indeed, the processual nature of a "wheel" defies a definitive, linear process.

The chakra system relies on the integrative nature of its multidimensionality, which again contradicts the suggestion of a hierarchal ranking among its component parts. Furthermore, each of us has our own spiritual path, governed in part by our karmic agreements, and we all have different energetic needs at different times. Thus, there is no singular way toward mastery, even though we all can benefit from the same tools on our journey.

Acknowledgements

I am deeply grateful for the support of all the beautiful souls who have entrusted me with their hearts in our work together. It is a gift to me to be able to be in service of your journey to self-acceptance and your truth. I am grateful for the endless support of my brilliant twin sister, Suzanne Zelazo, and for Ariel Patricia for her shared connection to Inanna and her masterful skill in helping people align with their destiny, as well as her profound vision and faith in me. I am grateful for Derek and Ryder Brucato—my beautiful, loving family, my all—who gave me the time and encouragement to complete this project and whose energy has helped me to become more balanced. I am indebted to the unconditional love and support of Tom Carmean as my ally in this life. I am thankful for the wise guidance of my father, Phil Zelazo; for the inspiration of my brother, Philip Zelazo; for my uncle, Jerry Burl, for his grace and courage in living and dying; and for Liz Varney, my soul sister with whom I walk this path and who generated important visual inspiration for this project. I am grateful for the profound knowledge and insight of Tricia McCannon, and to Christopher Patton for the fruitful and scholarly conversations about Inanna. I also want to thank Shasta Zaring, my exceptional teacher, for her wisdom, pure heart, courageous spirit, and magic, as well as all my teachers, past and present, and, of course, my sisterhood of fellow moon mamas. Finally, I would like to thank Madeleine Hay for her transcendent artwork throughout the book.

About the Author

Seana Zelazo is a psychotherapist, intuitive channel, spiritual coach, mentor, and teacher. A licensed clinical social worker who holds an MSW from the Smith College School for Social Work, Seana began her social work career in end-of-life care as a hospice social worker before transitioning into private practice as a psychotherapist. For the last decade, Seana has focused on providing clarity and support as an intuitive channel, connecting with the higher realms to offer guidance, spiritual coaching, and mentorship, as well as teaching. Trained in many healing modalities, Seana is also a former elite runner and two-time Olympic trials qualifier in the marathon, as well as a former competitive triathlete. As a surfer, today Seana uses her relationship to sports as a medium to be in sacred relationship with the temple of the body. She lives in coastal New Hampshire, where she surfs with her sisterhood year-round. This is her first book. Learn more at seanazelazo.com.

Endnotes

1 Wolkstein and Kramer, *Inanna, Queen of Heaven and Earth: Her Stories and Hymns from Sumer,* 12.

2 Eliot, T.S., *The Collected Poems and Plays- 1909-1950,* 144.

3 Kramer, *The Deluge,* in *The Ancient Near East Volume I,* ed, Pritchard, 28-30.

4 Poeble, A. *Publications of the Babylonian Section, Volume. IV, Historical Texts,* 7-70.

5 Kramer, *History Begins at Sumer,* 151.

6 -----, 151.

7 Among the foremost contributions to the study of sacred art as a portal to the Divine is William Henry, and I refer readers to his vast body of work including: https://courses.sacredstories.com/courses/rainbowlightbody.

8 Higginbotham, J., R., *Christo Paganism: An Inclusive Path,* 45.

9 Many teachers of ascension have brought to light the expansion of our chakra system to included 12 or 15 chakras which are becoming activated

through our evolutionary process. I refer you to the work of Diana Cooper and Tim Whild for further exploration, including their co-authored books, *The Archangel Guide to Ascension: 55 Steps to the Light* and *The Archangel Guide to Enlightenment and Mastery: Living in the Fifth Dimension*. However, the seven chakra system is used herein to align with Inanna's seven gates, and as a conceptual starting point for the process of evolution and ascension that Inanna's wisdom inspires.

10 The image of Inanna's Family Constellation is inspired by Inanna's family tree as depicted in Wolkstein and Kramer's *Inanna, Queen of Heaven and Earth*, x-xi.

11 The term "sinners" was originally a reference to moon worshippers.

12 See Kramer, *Sumerian Mythology: A Study of Spiritual and Literary Achievement in the Third Millennium B.C.,* xiv-xv.

13 Dumuzi is also known as Tammuz in his later iteration.

14 For example, Inanna standing facing her counselor Ninshubur with her foot upon the back of a lion in the ancient Akkadian cylinder seal of c. 2334-2154 BCE at The Oriental Institute Museum at the University of Chicago. Throughout the poetry of Enheduanna, Inanna is often referred to as a Lioness herself, or as riding one or many lions. See: *Lady of Largest Heart: Poems of the Sumerian High Priestess Enheduanna* by Betty De Shong Meador, p, 91, 119 and 125.

15 Meador, *Inanna: Lady of Largest Heart,* 45-46.

16 Stone, *When God Was a Woman,* 199-200.

17 Some scholars use the term *mes* as the plural for *me*, however, the author is honoring the translation done by Samuel Noah Kramer who was involved in its recovery.

18 Wolkstein and Kramer, *Inanna, Queen of Heaven and Earth*, 56.

19 Speiser, E. A., The Epic of Gilgamesh, *The Ancient Near East Volume I,* ed Pritchard. 40-75.

20 Wolkstein and Kramer, *Inanna, Queen of Heaven and Earth*, 60.

21 -----, 60.

22 -----, 66.

23 -----, 66.

24 Speiser, E. A., The Epic of Gilgamesh, *The Ancient Near East Volume I,* ed Pritchard. 40-75.

25 St. Germain is considered an ascended master who supports humanity in part through the wisdom and power of the violet flame—a powerful energy used to alchemize negative energy into positive energy.

26 Wolkstein and Kramer, *Inanna, Queen of Heaven and Earth, 12.*

27 Wolkstein and Kramer, *Inanna, Queen of Heaven and Earth, 14.* The word "grand" is an insertion by the author to clarify Enki's actual relationship to Inanna. Enki is Inanna's grandfather even though, as the text suggest, she is kind of a daughter figure to him.

28 -----, 14.

29 -----, 23.

30 -----, 24.

31 -----, 27.

32 -----, 24.

33 -----, 24.

34 -----, 24.

35 Kramer, *History Begins at Sumer*, 84-88.

36 -----, 155.

37 -----, 5.

38 -----, 143.

39 https://www.gatewaystobabylon.com/myths/texts/ninurta/mythanzu. htm accessed 12/28/21.

40 See for example, Tricia McCannon (https://courses.sacredstories. com/courses/treeoflife) as well as Denning and Phillips, *Magical States of Consciousness: Pathworking on the Tree of Life* and Hall, *The Secret Teachings of All Ages*.

41 Kramer, *Sumerian Mythology*, 34.

42 Deanne Anderson Lamont notes: "Ann Kilmer has described a Sumero-Akkadian game, *pukku-mekku* (ball and stick), which appears, at least on the surface, to have some similarities to field hockey and the Irish game of hurling." See Lamont, 208.

Endnotes

43 I refer the reader to *The Encyclopedia of Goddesses and Heroines,* by Patricia Monaghan (New World Library, Novato, California, 2014) for further exploration of various goddesses throughout the world.

44 For more information on the Akashic field, I refer readers to Ervin Laszlo's *Science and the Akashic Field: An Integral Theory of Everything,* Inner Traditions: Rochester, 2004.

45 Wolkstein and Kramer, *Inanna, Queen of Heaven and Earth, 31.*

46 -----, 31.

47 -----, 33.

48 -----, 33.

49 -----, 35.

50 -----, 36.

51 -----, 37.

52 -----, 37.

53 -----, 38.

54 -----, 39.

55 Also referred to as Agade, Akkad was a city in southern Mesopotamia, north of Sumer that was founded by King Sargon.

56 Wolkstein and Kramer, *Inanna, Queen of Heaven and Earth,* 38.

57 -----, 39.

58 McCannon, *The Return of the Divine Sophia: Healing the Earth Through the Lost Wisdom Teachings of Jesus, Isis, and Mary Magdalene*, 78-85.

59 Wolkstein and Kramer, *Inanna, Queen of Heaven and Earth*, 40.

60 Muhl, *The O Manuscript, 214.*

61 https://etcsl.orinst.ox.ac.uk/section1/tr133.htm (accessed April 23, 2022).

62 Bertrand and Bertrand, *Magdalene Mysteries, The Left-Hand Path of the Feminine Christ, 102.*

63 Wolkstein and Kramer, *Inanna, Queen of Heaven and Earth: Her Stories and Hymns from Sumer, 101.*

64 -----, 101.

65 -----, 101.

66 Wolkstein and Kramer, *Inanna, Queen of Heaven and Earth: Her Stories and Hymns from Sumer, 105.*

67 -----, 106.

68 -----, 106.

69 -----, 103.

70 -----, 103.

71 -----, 101.

72 -----, 103.

73 Frost, *The Poetry of Robert Frost*, 33.

Endnotes

74 Frost, *The Poetry of Robert Frost*, 34.

75 Wolkstein and Kramer, *Inanna, Queen of Heaven and Earth: Her Stories and Hymns from Sumer*, 103.

76 Freud, S. (1895) Draft H. Paranoia. *The Complete Letters of Sigmund Freud to Wilhelm Fliess, 1987-1904*, 107-112.

77 Wolkstein and Kramer, *Inanna, Queen of Heaven and Earth: Her Stories and Hymns from Sumer*, 97.

78 -----, 99.

79 -----, 99.

80 -----, 99.

81 -----, 99.

82 See Grahn, J. *Eruptions of Inanna: Justice, Gender, and Erotic Power,* and Roscoe, W. "Priests of the Goddess: Gender Transgression in Ancient Religion" in *History of Religions,* Vol 3. No. 3, February 1996.

83 Priest/ess is the author's linguistic construction to convey a non-binary, third term.

84 Muhl, *The O Manuscript, 83*

85 Meador, *Inanna: Lady of Largest Heart, 123*.

86 The phrase "I Am" refers to the "I Am" Discourses which were channeled by Saint Germain to Godfre Ray King in the 1930's. See King, G. R. *The "I Am" Discourses: Saint Germain Series, Volume 3*. Saint Germain Press, 2011 for further exploration.

87 Meador, *Inanna: Lady of Largest Heart*, 123-124.

88 Wolkstein and Kramer, *Inanna, Queen of Heaven and Earth: Her Stories and Hymns from Sumer*, 119.

89 -----, 70.

90 -----, 71.

91 -----, 71.

92 -----, 76.

93 -----, 75.

94 -----, 78.

95 -----, 83.

96 -----, 84.

97 -----, 88.

98 -----, 88.

99 -----, 89. Readers will notice the echo of this story in subsequent myths including its Mesopotamian version with Tammuz and Ishtar and the Greek myth of Demeter and Persephone.

100 Speiser, E. A, "The Epic of Gilgamesh" in *The Ancient Near East Volume I,* ed, Pritchard. 40-75.

101 -----, 53.

102 -----, 54.

103 Wolkstein and Kramer, *Inanna, Queen of Heaven and Earth: Her Stories and Hymns from Sumer*, 124.

104 https://www.heartmath.org/articles-of-the-heart/science-of-the-heart/the-energetic-heart-is-unfolding/

105 Van Der Kolk, B. *The Body Keeps the Score: Brain, Mind and Body in the Healing of Trauma*, 21.

106 Rinpoche, *Book of Living & Dying*, 92.

107 Meador, *Inanna: Lady of Largest Heart, 126-127.*

Bibliography

Bertrand, Seren and Bertrand, Azra. *Magdalene Mysteries, The Left-Hand Path of the Feminine Christ.* Rochester, VT: Bear & Company, 2020.

Cooper, D. & Whild, T. *The Archangel Guide to Ascension: 55 Steps to the Light.* NY, NY: Hay House, 2015.

Cooper, D. & Whild, T. *The Archangel Guide to Enlightenment and Mastery: Living in the Fifth Dimension.* NY, NY: Hay House, 2016.

Denning, M. & Phillips, O. *Magical States of Consciousness: Pathworking on the Tree of Life.* Woodbury: Llewellyn, 2012.

Eliot, T. S. *The Complete Poem and Plays: 1909-1950.* New York: Harcourt, Brace &World, Inc, 1971.

ETCSL (Electronic Text Corpus of Sumerian Literature). Oriental Institute, Oxford University (orinst.ox.ac.uk). https://etcsl.orinst.ox.ac.uk/section1/tr133.htm (accessed April 23, 2022).

Frost, R. *The Poetry of Robert Frost: All Eleven of His Complete Books.* New York: Holt, Rinehart and Winston, 1969.

Freud, S. (1895) Draft H. Paranoia. *The Complete Letters of Sigmund Freud to Wilhelm Fliess, 1987-1904.* tr. & ed. J. Masson. Cambridge: Belknap Press of Harvard University Press, 1985.

Godfre, Ray King. *The "I Am" Discourses: Saint Germain Series, Volume 3.* Schaumburg: Saint Germain Press, 2011.

Grahn, J. *Eruptions of Inanna: Justice, Gender, and Erotic Power.* New York: Nightboat Books, 2021.

Hall, M. *The Secret Teachings of All Ages.* New York: Penguin, 1984.

Higginbotham, J., R., *ChristoPaganism: An Inclusive Path.* Woodbury: Llewellyn, 2009.

Poebel, A. *Publications of the Babylonian Section, Volume IV, Historical Texts,* The University of Pennsylvania Museum: Philadelphia, 1914.

Jacobsen, Thorkild. *The Treasures of Darkness: A History of Mesopotamian Religion.* New Haven: Yale University Press, 1976.

Kramer, Samuel Noah. *Sumerian Mythology: A Study of Literary Achievement in The Third Millennium B.C.* Philadelphia: University of Pennsylvania Press, 1972.

Bibliography

Kramer, Samuel Noah. *History Begins at Sumer: Thirty-Nine Firsts in Recorded History,* Philadelphia: University of Pennsylvania Press, 1981.

Lamont, Deane Anderson. "Running Phenomena in Ancient Sumer." *Journal of Sport History* 22, no. 3 (1995): 207–15. http://www.jstor.org/stable/43610002.

Laszlo, Ervin. *Science and the Akashic Field: An Integral Theory of Everything,* Inner Traditions: Rochester, 2004.

McCannon, Trisha. *Return of the Divine Sophia, Healing the Earth Through the Lost Wisdom Teachings of Jesus, Isis, and Mary Magdalene.* Rochester, VT: Bear & Company, 2015.

Meador, Betty De Shong. *Inanna, Lady of Largest Heart: Poems of the Sumerian High Priestess Enheduanna.* Austin: University of Texas Press, 2009.

Monaghan, Patricia. *The Encyclopedia of Goddesses and Heroines,* Novato: New World Library, 2014.

Muhl, Lars. *The O Manuscript.* London: Watkins Publishing, 2013.

Pritchard, James, ed. *The Ancient Near East, Volume I.* Princeton University Press, 1958.

Pritchard, James, ed. *The Ancient Near East, Volume II.* Princeton University Press, 1975.

Rinpoche, Sogyal. *Tibetan Book of Living and Dying*. Harper San Francisco, 1993.

Roscoe, W. "Priests of the Goddess: Gender Transgression in Ancient Religion" in *History of Religions*, Vol. 35, No.3 (February, 1996), pp.195-230. The University of Chicago Press.

Stone, Merlin. *When God Was a Woman*, New York: Harcourt, 1976.

Van Der Kolk, MD. *The Body Keeps the Score: Brain, Mind and Body in the Healing of Trauma*. New York: Penguin, 2015.

Wolkstein, Diane and Kramer, Samuel. *Inanna, Queen of Heaven and Earth, Her Stories and Hymns from Sumer*. New York: Harper & Row, Publishers, 1983.